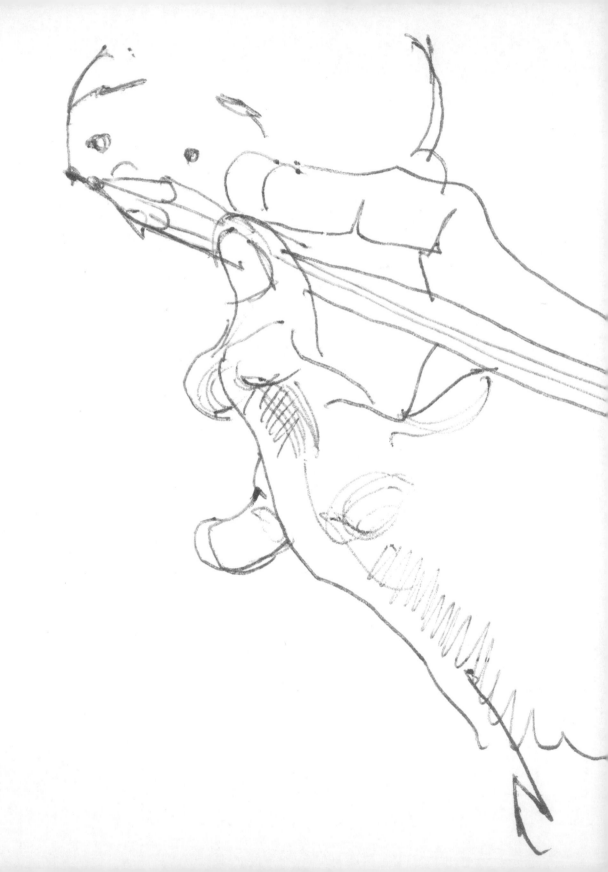

JUST JERRY

How Drawing Shaped My Life

A memoir by Caldecott Medalist

JERRY PINKNEY

ⓁⒷ

Little, Brown and Company

New York Boston

This book is a memoir. It reflects the author's recollections of his experiences at the time of writing. The author changed some names and characteristics when they could not be recalled and some events have been compressed or the timeline changed for literary purposes, and some dialogue has been re-created.

Little, Brown and Company • Hachette Book Group • 1290 Avenue of the Americas, New York, NY 10104
Visit us at LBYR.com • First Edition: January 2023 • Little, Brown and Company is a division of Hachette Book Group, Inc. The Little, Brown name and logo are trademarks of Hachette Book Group, Inc.

Library of Congress Cataloging-in-Publication Data
Names: Pinkney, Jerry, author, illustrator.
Title: Just Jerry : how drawing shaped my life / written and illustrated by Jerry Pinkney.
Description: First edition. | New York : Little, Brown and Company, 2023. | Audience: Ages 8–12 | Summary: "Jerry Pinkney, Caldecott Medal winner and illustrator of over one hundred books, tells the story of his childhood and how he developed his artistic talent" —Provided by publisher.
Identifiers: LCCN 2022022389 | ISBN 9780316383851 (hardcover)
Subjects: LCSH: Pinkney, Jerry—Juvenile literature. | Illustrators—United States—Biography—Juvenile literature. | African American illustrators—Biography—Juvenile literature.
Classification: LCC NC975.5.P56 A2 2023 | DDC 741.6/42092 [B] —dc23/eng/20220623
LC record available at https://lccn.loc.gov/2022022389
ISBNs: 978-0-316-38385-1 (hardcover) • 978-0-316-38384-4 (ebook)
Printed in China • APS • 10 9 8 7 6 5 4 3 2 1

CONTENTS

Editor's Note

Jerry Pinkney, the author and illustrator of this work, passed away on October 20, 2021. While his work on this text was nearly finished at that time—after well over a decade of writing and rewriting—only sketches for the final artwork had been completed. Jerry had envisioned the published book to contain more than a hundred detailed graphite drawings. Between chapters, he'd planned wordless visual sequences with several panels per page, in the spirit of a graphic novel, each section of drawings setting the stage for the next story he was about to share. In addition, select standalone images were to be placed within and at the end of each chapter.

It was an ambitious goal, and one that he would have accomplished with his typical precision and indefatigable energy. The project was a labor of love for him, and in collaboration with his wife and creative partner of more than sixty years, Gloria Jean Pinkney, he was able to tackle the challenge of bringing his story to life even as he created many classic picture books, mentored a new generation of artists, inspired children at school visits, and helped raise a cherished family, many of whom pursued work in the creative arts.

It is fortunate that Jerry was a consummate draftsman who always had a sketchbook close at hand from the earliest age, for many of his rough drawings alone are accomplished enough to carry the weight of his personal story, and compellingly bring to life the internal and external worlds of a boy who passionately loved to draw. This book has been visually composed in a way that differs from Jerry's intention but hopefully still captures his goal.

During a decade of talking about and working on this project, Jerry made it clear that his goal was to believably bring readers into the world in which he grew up, on an all-Black block in Philadelphia called East Earlham Street, and a visually immersive approach was part of his plan to achieve that. Another choice he made was to recall the language typical of the post–World War II era, such as the use of "Colored" in thoughts and dialogue, which is how both Black and white people of the time usually referred to African Americans. Any other term would have lacked authenticity for Jerry and those familiar with the era. And finally, it was Jerry's hope that this book would also be friendly to readers with dyslexia, and to that end the body text is set in a font specifically designed for that purpose. We have also found many opportunities to shorten and vary line lengths to help such readers keep track as they read.

Together, Jerry's heartfelt words and distinctive, detailed sketches vividly bring to life the story of a young artist growing up in the 1940s and '50s, making his way slowly but surely toward his future as a beloved, legendary illustrator.

Jerry's studio: Now

m house
tub, John [no sink]
eut father's workshe
ce and coal ben
back of house

bedroom

bath

Hall landing

bedroom   Hall

bed room

work bench

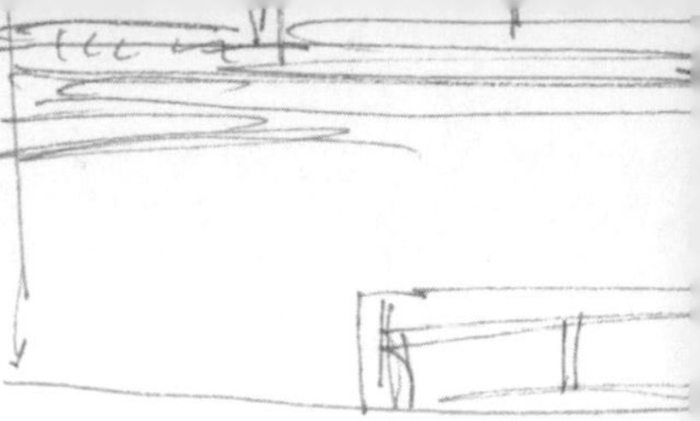

cold shutt

One the thing
as an adult is ho
However as a ch
much about it.
street with home
The other side
51 Seem at th
CAR / Ford

back yard

shead

kitchen

Dining room

Living room

On Drawu
Places in the
to draw
a: my bedr
I can sti
in my roon
calling for
b: We hade
room and
under the
and paper

I was all
Some gui

al shutte

ment

aw thinks that had
ucks and especially
wold also get the model 3in
the one were you build
plawd, the mater elwhere
and glue.) and painstaking
plane most often war plane
I was somthing I did with my brothes

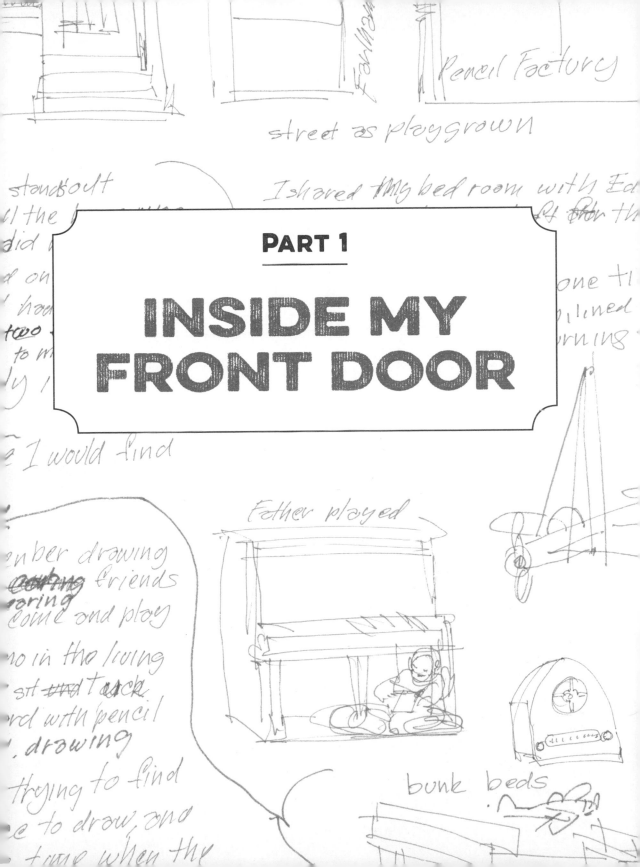

street as playground

Pencil Factory

standsout

I shared my bedroom with Ed

e I would find

Father played

bunk beds

PART 1
INSIDE MY FRONT DOOR

CHAPTER 1

THROUGH THE BACK DOOR

Philadelphia could get pretty sticky in late August, but the summer of 1949, when I was nine years old, the city was hot as fire. And if you couldn't sleep, it seemed even hotter. My bedroom was furnace-like, with one little window facing the alley, too small to allow for even a breeze to squeeze through.

During the day it could feel much worse, with the sun beating down on people, cars, buildings, concrete sidewalks, and cobblestone and asphalt streets. Even on the hottest days, my buddies and I—Bobby, Elsworth, and Alfred—loved to gallop at full speed through our crowded block, pretending to be on horseback like the adventurous cowboys we dreamed of being. Here on East Earlham Street, we had to dodge family and neighbors at every turn—whether it was my sisters and their friends jumping double-Dutch, Uncle Alec slowly polishing the cab of his cross-country trailer, families hand-cranking homemade ice cream and root beer, or thick clusters of men and women catching up on the local news.

"Slow down, young'uns, before you hurt somebody!" our neighbor Miss Sadie called out to us, as she often did. She was a daily presence, a silhouetted figure behind her screen door, keeping

her eyes on everyone. Her voice was so loud we could hear it over the shouts of hucksters, car engines, and whinnying horses pulling wagons loaded down with fruits and vegetables.

We didn't always like people such as Miss Sadie looking in on what we were doing. Yet the grown-ups on East Earlham Street acted like kinfolk—loving us, scolding us, and, above all, doing their best to protect us. These were folks who *saw* us. They didn't look *through* us, like many of the white people on Germantown and Chelten Avenues. On our tight-knit, all-Black block, we felt cared for. In 1940s and 1950s Philadelphia, East Earlham Street was one of the only places I knew where every face looked like mine.

Grandma Clara and Granddad Charles's house was at the end of the block, and their living room window overlooked the gas lamppost my buddies and I liked to climb. I made sure that Grandma Clara didn't see us as we shimmied up the pole. Grandma had a stare of disapproval that was far worse than fear of a scolding or spanking. It was even more painful than when Mr. Scott, my arithmetic teacher, struck his ruler across the palm of my hand when I accidentally reversed numbers. That was something that happened to me a lot.

One by one, we heaved ourselves from the pole and over the iron fencing and poison ivy vines covering the stone-and-concrete wall enclosing Saint Luke's Episcopal Church Cemetery, which turned East Earlham's narrow street into a dead end. White folks didn't buy houses on a block closed in by a cemetery because it wasn't considered a nice place to raise a family, but that made the houses on East Earlham affordable for folks like us.

We dropped down into the old cemetery and tore off along the length of my grandparents' house. I was usually faster than Bobby, but when I glanced over my shoulder, I saw him just behind me.

"Giddy-up! Yee-haw!" yelled Elsworth and Alfred as they tried to catch us.

I leaped back onto the wall and then scrambled atop the roof of my grandparents' chicken coop, scattering the chickens. Then

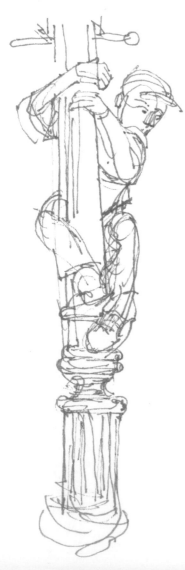

I jumped down, landing in their backyard. With Bobby at my heels, I scooted into the alley.

"Gotcha!" said Bobby, tagging me. He made circling movements over his head with his other arm, like he was throwing a lasso. "Stay where you are," he shouted.

I fake-stumbled and fell to my knees. "Aw, man," I muttered, "I quit!"

"Good Lord, what's that ruckus?" Grandma Clara called from her kitchen.

Just then Elsworth and Alfred showed up. "We better get out of here," they said, then took off with Bobby. I hurried toward home, knowing that Mother would already have supper on the table.

Out of breath, I reached the backyard of

51 East Earlham Street, brushed dirt off my khakis, tucked in my shirt, and pushed open our wobbly old gate. It creaked loudly, announcing my late arrival.

My yard, like all those on our block, was small, with trash stacked on one side and things to be saved, like Mother's plant pots, on the other. I made my way through a forest of laundry on the clothesline to the door of the shed—a small, cluttered back room of the house that was never locked.

Before I could reach the kitchen door, I had to squeeze by all the stuff that couldn't fit anywhere else in our tiny house: an icebox, Mother's washing machine and clothes wringer, laundry baskets, and large glass jugs of spring water. The aroma of tonight's dinner was wafting out: pork chops, collard greens, and sweet potatoes. I could even smell that a peach cobbler, my favorite dessert, was baking in the oven.

51 Earlwood Street Phillip

I wanted to head straight to my room and sketch out all the adventures spinning around in my head from the movie I'd just watched at the cinema with my buddies: Roy Rogers, cowboys with lassos, wild horses to break and bad guys to catch. But my youngest sister, Helen; my older sister, Joan; and my middle sister, Claudia, were already at the kitchen table waiting for me. Mother always insisted that her four youngest eat together.

"Where have you been?" Joan asked, rolling her eyes. "You're late again! You're always either upstairs with that sketchpad or running around playing cowboys with those homeboys of yours!"

I froze in my tracks. Confrontations made me uneasy, especially with people whom I was close to, like my sisters. I was relieved when Claudia jumped in. "You're not our boss, Joan!" Helen cupped her hand over her mouth, trying not to giggle. "You're just still mad at Jerry for drawing that picture of you sleeping on the couch, when you were supposed to be taking care of me and Helen."

"Jerry!" Mother called from
her reading chair in the living room, where
she used to read fables and fairy tales to me when I was younger, and
where she now waited for Dad and my two brothers to come home
from work. "Wash your hands and sit down before supper gets cold."

"Yes, go wash your hands," Joan added, "*Jerry*-with-a-nickname-
and-no-middle-name!"

Joan knew her remark would sting me. I had been teased by kids
in school about my name. Whenever there was a new teacher, I'd often
been asked, "What is your *real* name? Jerry is a nickname." One of my
teachers had even written "Gerald Pinkney" on my report card.

Mother closed her book and walked in. "Joan," she said sternly,
"just 'Jerry' is enough. He'll make something of that name." Mother

always had a way of making me, her youngest son, believe that I would grow up to be more than "just Jerry."

"I like Jerry's name, *and* his pictures," said Helen. "I don't know anyone else that can draw as good as he can."

"Well," Joan had to admit grumpily, "the last thing you said is true!"

"Let's just eat in peace," Claudia added. I washed my hands and sat down, staring at my plate. We all ate without saying another word.

But after supper, when we were cleaning up, Claudia began teasing Joan, who was still pouting. "Knock it off!" Joan hollered, pinching Claudia's arm. Helen called for Mother to make them stop. Everyone talked at the same time, each sister raising her voice louder and louder.

This wasn't an unfamiliar sound in our six-room house, filled with my seven other boisterous family members, but it always caused my stomach to knot and my legs to feel shaky. Why did they have to yell? Even Mother's reassuring voice was drowned out.

Sometimes life in our house felt like being jerked around on Snap the Whip at Willow Grove Park, a ride I hated because it made me feel so out of control. Soon Dad and my older brothers, Eddie and Billy, would be home, adding their booming voices, making our little house feel even smaller. Even so, we never really dreamed about living in a larger house, because we were the lucky ones: We lived on the side of the street with homes that had three bedrooms. The other side of the street had only two-bedroom homes.

"Be right back," I mumbled, without any plans to return. I slipped into the narrow hallway, stacked high with wooden crates of fruits and vegetables that Dad had stored there for the next day of huckstering, one of his many jobs.

Climbing the stairs, I headed to the bedroom in the back of the house that I shared with Eddie and Billy. Even with the door shut, I could hear all the chaos going on below in the kitchen. I sank down on the lower bunk with a sketchpad and flipped through the pages of pictures: Mother's potted plants, knights in armor, countless fighter planes, and yesterday's drawing of Joan sleeping on the couch.

"Dag," I said under my breath, "was she mad when I showed it to Mother and Dad!" It was proof that she had been sleeping on the job. Next there were pages and pages of favorite comic book characters: Billy the Kid, Hopalong Cassidy, and the Lone Ranger.

I'd been drawing for as far back as I could remember. My grand-father Charles worked at the Blaisdell pencil factory on the corner of East Earlham and Lena Streets, so there was no shortage of pencils around. Drawing was the one thing I felt I could do right, the one thing people told me I was good at. It was my way of living in my imagination, and breaking free of the constraints I was growing up with. Every-thing I saw, heard, felt, tasted, and smelled, I'd think of as a picture. When I wasn't sketching, I was just gathering and storing up experi-ences into a visual memory bank, ready to be translated to paper. It

was as if I had a compartment in my brain that held a sketchbook and my granddad's pencils.

After grabbing one of the pencils from an empty mayonnaise jar, I added more lines to a cowboy on horseback. They flowed out of my hand without my even trying, carrying me far away to the limitless plains of the West.

At long last, I heard only the comforting scratching of my pencil on paper; everything was quiet in my head. Finally, I was alone, able to be anything and go anywhere.

And in the world in which I was living, to be anything or go any-where was not a dream that young Black boys often dared to have.

CHAPTER 2

DOWN THE
BASEMENT STAIRS

My buddies and I often hung out at the vacant lot next door to our younger friend Sonny's house and directly across from Grandma Clara and Grandpa Charles's place. We parked our bikes there, claiming that space as our own hangout. It's also where we built go-carts, and shoeshine boxes for when we'd shine shoes to earn some pocket change. One day, Elsworth came up with the idea to build a clubhouse.

"That would be too hard," Sonny complained.

"We could build it out of the wooden boards left over from the old fence over there," I told him, pointing to the other side of the lot.

"That's a great idea," said Elsworth.

We all scoured the alleyways and streets nearby for whatever we could find—worn-down fencing, red bricks from crumbling buildings and sidewalks. "There's an abandoned car near the Armat train station," Alfred told us. "We could get a window from it. Wouldn't that be cool?"

"We could pry it out with Dad's crowbar," I added.

After that, our days were spent gathering stuff for building and hauling it back to the lot. "All we need now," said Elsworth finally, "is tools. Can we borrow your Dad's saw and hammers? We're gonna need nails, too."

"Yeah, man," I responded. "Dad won't mind, as long as we put them back before he needs them. My ol' man can be fussy about his tools."

I had worked beside Dad on his home-repair job sites, ripping down walls and putting up new ones, so I figured I knew how to build a clubhouse. I wondered if Dad would be proud of me for that. I always wanted to please him. Dad was a talkative man with an open smile who loved to hug, but I wasn't usually the one receiving his embrace. I loved to watch him around other people, though. He had an energy and sense of purpose and pride in himself that drew people to him.

I bounded down the street and into our house and immediately noticed how quiet it was. No one was dancing, laughing, or squabbling. In the living room, the record player—perched on top of the ironing board for lack of another place to store it—was turned off, since Joan was

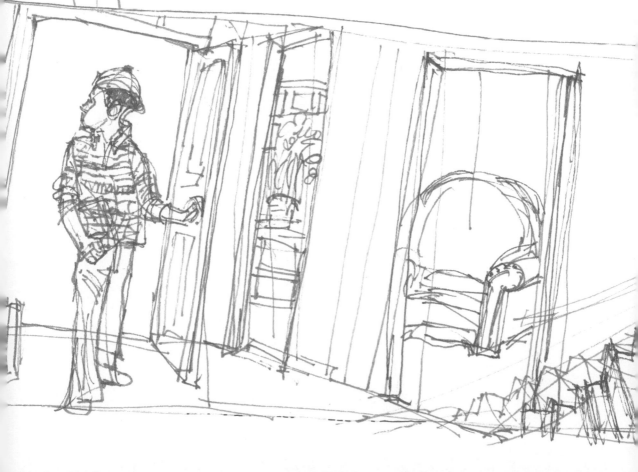

at after–school band rehearsal. Mother, who was a day worker and caretaker for a young child, had left the house early that morning. My oldest brother, Eddie, and Dad were house painting, and Billy was working at his after–school job unloading produce for the Acme Supermarket.

I opened the door to the cellar and clicked on the light to Dad's workshop. Mother had warned us, "Don't go downstairs without your father. There are too many ways that you could get hurt!"

But I didn't want to disappoint my friends. *I'll be extra careful,*

I decided. To me, Dad's workshop was the most magical place in the world. He was a handyman by trade, but he was a craftsman to me, and his basement was like his studio.

The first thing that hit me was a mixture of different smells: dampness from peeling walls; chunks of coal in the coalbin, left over from last winter; sawdust on the floor; and empty paint cans now filled with the turpentine Dad used for cleaning paint brushes. The odors made me feel a little dizzy. The only light was from the half window, where a metal chute was placed during coal deliveries. The dim light and shadows made the basement feel eerie.

Did something move? I wondered anxiously. I had a pretty active imagination, and it didn't take much to get me nervous. *Of course not,* I tried to reassure myself, knowing that everything in Dad's workshop, even the shadows, belonged to him.

It was only once I'd pulled the chain to turn on the bare bulb dangling over Dad's workbench that I could breathe normally. Now I could see ribbons of color bouncing off shiny copper tubing and new gallons of paint. Fresh lumber was neatly stacked along the wall. Dad had everything organized: leftover wallpaper, wallpaper catalogs, tubes of paint, mixing sticks, brushes, electrical wire, hacksaws, wood saws, hammers, nails, screwdrivers, and screws. His workspace was a world of its own—a sanctuary where he built things; mixed colors; fixed broken lamps, appliances, and radios; and refinished old furniture until the surfaces looked new.

Dad's workbench was a fantastic arena of tools illuminated by the hanging lamp, which cast a perfect circle-shaped beam like the spotlight at a circus. In my mind's eye I saw the tools come to life like performers taming lions or acrobats swinging on a trapeze. Dad's precision and skill weren't much different to me than incredible acrobatic feats, and I wanted to have those powers, too. But I often felt pretty clumsy around Dad. I always wondered how he could remember what each tool was for, and how he'd managed to teach himself to use so many of them.

Mounted on one side of his table was a wood lathe; on the other side was a vise. On the wall behind his bench was a pegboard with other tools, including the saw we needed. After securing the hammers from his tool belt, I carefully lifted a handsaw from its hook, making sure that I didn't disturb anything Dad had been working on, especially the old radio chassis, which looked as if he'd just walked away from it moments ago.

Gripping the saw created in me a sense of connection with him, as if he were right beside me. It took me back to the day earlier that week when Dad had laid a four-inch pine board across two sawhorses to teach me to cut. Using a straightedge, he'd drawn a guideline with a flat yellow pencil.

"This is a carpenter's pencil," he'd told me. "Now, hold the saw with your elbow bent. Keep the saw teeth on the line. Remember," he'd added, with a wrinkled brow and a stern voice, "the teeth are sharp!" He hadn't forgotten how last time we'd done this together, I'd nicked myself and drawn blood.

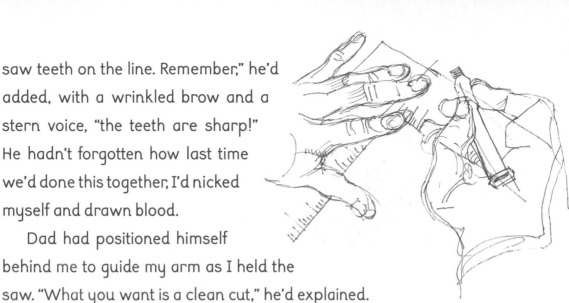

Dad had positioned himself behind me to guide my arm as I held the saw. "What you want is a clean cut," he'd explained.

Focus, I'd reminded myself. *Don't look at Dad to see if he approves. Keep your eyes on what you're doing.* Sawdust had floated to the floor as I made even, back-and-forth movements.

"When you get close to the end of the cut, hold on to the wood," Dad had said. "Don't let it break off and drop. That would leave your board with splinters. You don't want that, do you?" he'd added, shaking his head.

"No, sir," I'd responded, echoing Dad's serious tone. When it was finished, Dad had held my board up to the light, then stacked it with the other planks he'd cut.

Did that mean that mine was as good as the others?

"Now I need to call one of my customers," he'd told me, heading up the stairs. "I hope that with all this party-line nonsense, I'll be able to get a call through without having to ask Miss Sadie how

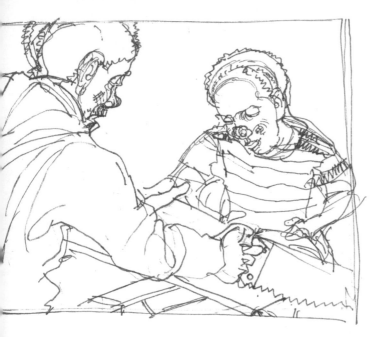

soon she's going to free up the line!"

"Dad," I'd called as he opened the door, "how did I do?"

The door shut. *"Dad,"* I'd called again, *"how did I do? Was it a clean cut?"*

No answer.

Dad's silence reminded me of how he used to give me scraps of leftover wallpaper from his jobs so I could draw on the blank sides, but he never took the time to look at the drawings I made on them.

"Focus," I said again, aloud this time, bringing me back to the present. "The guys are waiting for these tools!"

I looked around for the other things we needed and spotted sheets of blue drafting paper with rough sketches for one of Dad's projects. I had seen him drawing up plans for the house that Uncle Osbie and Aunt Helen were building in New Jersey, with the help of Mother's sisters and their husbands.

It gave me another idea.

Carefully I removed a blank sheet and folded it until it fit into my sketchpad. Next, I grabbed nails and carpenter pencils out of the toolbox. "We're going to need these, too."

Before shutting off the light, I made sure that the rest of Dad's tools were exactly as he left them. With hammers, crowbar, saw, straight-edge, and nails, and with my sketchpad tucked under an arm, I climbed the stairs, barely making it to the kitchen table without dropping anything.

Inspired by the workshop, I took the sketchpad to one of my favorite places to draw: beneath the keyboard of our upright piano. It was one of the few spaces in the house that felt sheltered. The doors of our home weren't locked during the day, so everyone from the ice man to relatives and friends could just walk in, and they did. There was no private space, so I'd created my own little art studio.

The piano was painted with the same pink paint that Dad, Billy, and

Eddie used for the entire living room. Using its stool as a desk, I made some quick sketches with Dad's carpenter pencil of building plans for the clubhouse.

"Jerry, aw, man!" I suddenly heard Bobby yell from outside the window. "Are you drawing under that piano again? When are you coming out? Do you know how long—"

"Bobby," I interrupted, "you're just in time. Come in and gimme some help! You take the straightedge, nails, and hammers. I'll carry the rest."

Bobby grumbled all the way back to the lot.

"Got everything but my ol' man's sawhorses," I told Alfred and Sonny. "We can go back to get them later. Come on over to Sonny's stoop."

Once there I unfolded the drafting paper, smoothed it out, and began showing off my ideas for the clubhouse. I would make it a building that Dad would be proud of.

CHAPTER 3

ON THE
SECOND FLOOR

Though World War II had ended five years earlier, its shadow still hung over us. I learned most of what I knew about it—and about the "Cold War" with Russia that we were experiencing now—through short news clips shown at the movies right before the cartoons and the feature films. My parents didn't like to talk about the war, but I wanted to know everything—all about the planes and the battles and the heroes.

I'd built a wide assortment of model planes with my older brother Billy, who dreamed of becoming a pilot. My buddies and I loved picturing ourselves sitting in cockpits in dogfights, pretending to be brave, just like the pilots we saw in the movies. I liked to draw fighter planes looping and diving in aerial combat, climbing up through the clouds, their propellers spinning so fast you could hardly make out the shape. To us, in our small world on East Earlham Street, war seemed like the ultimate adventure.

Until one evening, when I discovered a stack of *Life* magazines from World War II buried under Mother's bed linens inside a large wardrobe on the second floor. *Why would Mother and Dad put them here?* I wondered. *What don't they want us kids to see?* Living so close together, we didn't have a lot of secrets in our house, so anything that seemed intentionally hidden from view made me especially curious.

After making sure no one was coming, I grabbed some magazines with sweaty palms, then crept into my room and eased the door shut. I climbed onto the top bunk, pushing the blanket aside so that I could slide the magazines out of sight if needed.

With shallow breaths I stared at a photo of a sailor in the same uniform that my brother Eddie, now serving in the Navy, was wearing when he came home on his first break from military service. Trying to read some of the headlines was hard, since the letters always turned backward and tripped me up. So instead I turned to a section with mostly photos.

Flipping through the pages with shaky hands, I stared at photographs of figures lying facedown in murky waters on a beach in the country of Burma, of the bombing of Pearl Harbor in Hawaii, of burning planes, of running soldiers and sailors, and of German prisoners of war walking in lockstep with their hands clasped on their heads. One photograph showed lines of bone-thin children and adults in ragged, striped uniforms behind wire fences, and so many sad faces that it made me shiver. *Could these kids be my age?* I asked myself. Yet some of the people were smiling, too. Slowly I sounded out the headline: THEY HAVE LANDED—HOW D-DAY LED TO LIBERATION.

Instead of pictures of soldiers standing tall and looking proud, I saw men who seemed beaten down or in pain. Instead of faces smiling in victory at the war's end, I saw starved people in rags being led out of camps. Though they had survived the enemy's cruelty, they looked like ghosts.

I didn't want to see any more. So I gathered all the magazines and quietly put them back just as they had been. Even after I closed the drawer, the horrible images stuck with me.

I dove into bed early. With blankets over my head, I was able to cover up the noises coming up the stairwell from the TV, but I could not shut out the *Life* magazine photographs of the children behind the wire fence. They would later surface in my mind during our school air-raid drills, and on nights when I found it difficult to sleep I would see images of plumes of smoke, thin faces, and frail bodies.

Lying in the dark, I could see how the light from the hallway cast shadows in the room, making everything a little eerie. Everywhere I looked, it seemed something was hiding, out to get me. The tower of wrinkled clothes became a spooky creature from outer space, lurching toward me on four skinny wooden legs. The open closet door became a dark, scary hole. Behind it, the wire hangers looked like skeletons. I thought of the people I had seen in the magazine earlier, with their bony faces and hollowed eyes, and I shuddered.

The only relief came when I began drawing on the wall beside my bunk. It was something I did from time to time when I wanted to escape the world. Real life was scary, but in drawing, I felt safe. I would invite everything I experienced—all of my senses—to visit with me in that special space of the imagination. It didn't even matter that I was sketching over my old drawings. It only mattered that I was making pictures. Gradually, with each stroke I made, the images of the children behind the wire fence faded away.

Billy came up the stairs and into the bedroom, switching the

light on. He was holding the model plane we'd just finished building together.

"Hey," he said in his baritone voice, surprised to see me in bed.

"Hey right back to you," I responded.

"Is something troubling you?" he asked. "Why are you in bed so early? Why aren't you downstairs watching TV with Mother and the girls, or hanging out in the basement with Dad?"

"Just thinking," I replied, and he smiled at my familiar answer.

Billy held up the model. "This plane will be part of our collection," he said, fumbling around in the top bureau drawer. "There's string and tacks somewhere in here…."

I watched Billy as he hung the new plane. He was so tall that he had no problem reaching the ceiling. "What a collection we've put together!" he remarked.

Afterward he sat down on the lower bunk. "I have reading to do," he told me. "I've got to get ready for the Temple University entrance exam. Mother thinks I should consider going to college. But today, my teacher told our class about the Tuskegee Airmen. They're Colored pilots who are flying fighter planes. So maybe the Air Force is a better idea. Although Eddie really likes the Navy, especially since President Truman integrated the Armed Forces. Anyway," he added, "if I continued my education, what would I do then? Go to work in a factory?"

I wasn't sure if Billy was talking to me or to himself. "You got that right!" I responded. I didn't have any idea what he should do. I didn't have any idea what I should do someday, either.

"Jerry," said Billy, like he was reading my mind, "what do you want to do when you graduate from school?"

"I don't know," I responded. "I guess I'll just do what Dad does." Then I found a blank space on the wall to squeeze in another drawing of airplanes and soldiers.

The next day, I returned from school to find Dad's ladder and a can of white paint outside my door. Entering the room, I noticed that the wall next to my bunk had been freshly painted. All of the drawings I'd made there were gone.

My heart sank. I didn't care about the pictures, but I was worried about Dad. Was he mad that I had marked up the wall?

Dad usually arrived home around six thirty, and that day, I sat outside anxiously waiting for him on the front stoop. I always suspected that Dad thought of my art as a useless pastime, that he wondered why I would spend so much time lost in the pages of a sketchbook when I should be preparing for something more serious.

As soon as he got out of his car, I ran to him and blurted, "Dad, are you sore with me for drawing on the wall?"

Dad smiled. "No, Jerry," he said. "I just thought you needed a clean space to draw more pictures." Then he went into the house without another word.

I skipped stairs all the way up to my room to draw some more. This time, I drew for fun: Mighty Mouse, Tom and Jerry, and Bugs Bunny. Trucks and trains and knights at a round table. Pirate ships on the high seas. And castles, like I had seen in the Arabian Nights movies. I drew myself in the middle of the action, ready to fight. I was the master of all of the monsters!

My pencil felt like a sword in my hand, and that night, I fell asleep still holding it.

41

neighborhood had it's own we d

venture very far. I do remember

ewea some boxin's instruction.

the wall was taken down

built a boys club house

in dilapidated houses.

to be all

our

with wood from

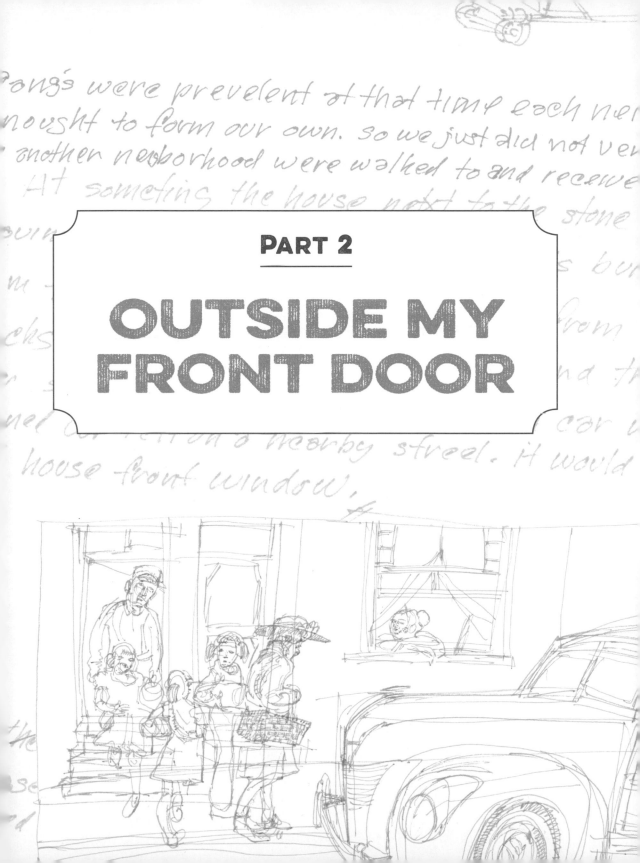

PART 2

OUTSIDE MY FRONT DOOR

CHAPTER 4

SURVIVING AT SCHOOL

Weekday mornings were always hectic at our house, especially because there was only one bathroom, with a tub but no sink. Even with Eddie gone in the Navy, there were still seven of us who had to find a way to wash up under the tub faucet, taking turns.

One Friday morning, after everyone was dressed, I was sitting at the kitchen table, not in the least bit hungry. I was frowning over my school textbook instead. I always struggled the most with writing, with the way the words twisted until they didn't make sense.

Mother got up from her chair after tying ribbons in Helen's hair. "Perfect," she said, humming "Blessed Assurance," her favorite spiritual.

All the sounds of early morning buzzed around me—doors slamming, dishes clattering in the sink, footsteps charging up and down the stairs, overlapping voices of five kids getting ready for school—so I didn't hear Mother come up right behind me.

"Stomachache again?" she whispered in my ear. I nodded, wondering how she always seemed to know exactly how I was feeling.

"Let's see if we can make that hurting go away," she said gently. Friday was the day we took English tests at school. That morning, as on other Fridays, Mother reached into her pocket and took out a pack of Tums, placing two tablets in my hand.

Her voice and her touch comforted me. Mother always knew when I needed to feel better about myself. Around Mother, I felt valuable, that all things were possible. I slipped the Tums in my pocket, picked up my schoolbooks and sketchpad, then headed out the door.

East Earlham Street was continuously in motion. Everything and everybody was moving toward Lena Street, which was the only way out of our dead end. Adults were leaving for work, and East Earlham's kids were on the way to school. With all the houses snuggled so close together, our block always felt like a beehive—pulsating, crowded, and noisy. Soon delivery men would be leaving their orders of milk and bread on doorsteps, and hucksters would be hawking their produce.

I popped the Tums in my mouth and called to Bobby, Elsworth, and Sonny, "Wait up!"

What we saw during the walk from East Earlham Street to Joseph E. Hill Elementary School reminded me of the crates of fruits and vegetables that Dad stored in our hallway when he was a huckster: apples in one crate, peaches in another, melons in their own wooden box. It was much like that with the local people, and the color of their skin. Black people could live only in certain sections, and white people lived in others.

In those days, Philly was not as plainly segregated as many of the Southern cities, but there was often still an implied separation of the races—a limit on where we could go, things we could do, who we could talk to. Stores did not have any WHITES ONLY signs posted, but the OPEN or WELCOME signs on doors didn't always mean that my friends and I really could enter and be served.

One day I'd overheard Mother talking to Miss Sadie about how my parents had enrolled me, Eddie, Billy, and Joan at Hill Elementary, where all the teachers and students were Black.

"Even though there weren't many schools that would hire Colored teachers," she said, "Hill hired the best!" By the time Claudia and Helen started school, my parents had decided that attending schools with both Black and white students was a good thing. "It was one of the reasons our families left the South and moved north," Mother explained. I wished she'd say more to us about that—anytime I asked my parents about what life was like for my family down South, they found a way to change the subject. "So, in 1950," Mother went on, "we had Claudia and Helen attend mixed schools with all white teachers, because of course Colored teachers were not permitted to teach white students."

Walking to school that Friday—with my head down and my stomach churning, thinking only of the dreaded English test—I lagged behind the other boys. But at least I was heading to a place where my teachers understood the community I was coming from.

"Hey, Jerry, don't be a slowpoke," Alfred called out.

At the corner of Germantown and Chelten Avenues we met up with other schoolmates. We greeted one another with raised hands and quick jabs, mimicking boxers Joe Louis and Sugar Ray Robinson as we moved along the avenue. I'd taken boxing lessons at the Police Athletic League, so I was pretty good at pretend fighting. We didn't stop sparring until we reached the entrance of the Vernon Theatre.

All of us were excited about the next double feature of Western films, and we began reading the posters aloud. It was hard for me to keep up reading with my buddies, and I hated being left behind as they raced through the words, so I faked it: I watched Bobby's eyes and the shape of his lips as he spoke, and then copied him. I'd been doing this for so many years that I was good at it, and did it without thinking much about it. Even though I skipped over some of the words, no one could tell but me. Somehow, we all ended up at the same place at the same time.

As we walked on, the guys played a game of reading window signs out loud, and in the same way, I pretended to join in. They didn't quiet down until we turned onto Rittenhouse Street and into the schoolyard. We split up just as the first bell rang.

I ran to my classroom and sank into my seat, feeling miserable all over again. Our room was noisy, with my classmates slamming their books and pencils on the desks, but when Mrs. Miller stood up, the room grew quiet.

"Boys and girls," she announced, "you have forty-five minutes before your test to review your English workbooks. Open them now and begin. The only sound in our classroom should be the clock on the wall."

I froze up during much of the study period. *Why am I feeling so tired?* I constantly wondered. *And why is the* tick-tock, tick-tock *of that clock louder than ever?*

I thought back on so many years of Thursday evenings, reviewing the list of words I'd be quizzed on and trying to mentally hold on to their spellings. Years of reading page after page, chapter after chapter; thinking I might've finally captured a sentence's meaning, only to lose it as I drifted off over the homework, eyelids heavy with the effort. Of course, once I went up to bed I'd be wide awake again, anxiety keeping me up.

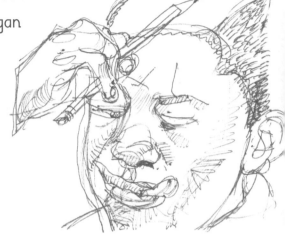

I felt like I'd had no time at all to study before Mrs. Miller began handing out the test pages. My chest tightened with dread even when Mrs. Miller smiled at me as she placed a sheet on my desk.

"Bring your papers up front when you finish," she told the class. "Then you're dismissed for recess."

When I looked down at the pages, the words seemed to be swimming in murky water. It was as if the paper was already soggy, and I'd only just begun. Even when I gripped my paper, the words kept moving.

It was hard enough to grasp single words, but there were whole paragraphs I needed to understand. I tried different ways to figure out their meaning: *Don't get bogged down because you can't read every last word....Skip the words that you can't sound out....If you can string together enough words that you do know, maybe you can get what the whole sentence means.*

Each time I recognized a word, a

feeling of relief came over me. But too often that led to more questions, and every time that happened, I had to start over again. And that was just reading. Writing was another challenge, especially spelling. I'd have one word in my head, then write another word instead.

"Focus, focus, focus," I mumbled under my breath.

Anxiously I looked around to see if any of my classmates were still at their desks. Right then my friend Jennifer smiled at me on her way to turn her papers in. Quickly, I folded my papers in half so she couldn't see all the questions I was unable to answer.

Now I was the only student left in the room. Reluctantly, I handed my paper to the teacher, saying, "I tried, Mrs. Miller."

"I know you did, Jerry," she responded with a reassuring smile. "You're a smart young man. We must try to figure out what is making classwork so challenging for you. I don't want you to be pulled out of my class and sent to special education classes again, with no one knowing how to help. Let me think about it," she added. "And come back early from recess."

My classmates were horsing around in the schoolyard. Without being spotted, I jammed my hands into my pants pockets and made my way to the chain-link fence, the miserable test still on my mind until it was time for me to go back inside.

"Sit down, Jerry," said Mrs. Miller. "I'll be with you in in a second."

Mrs. Miller reminded me of Mother. I didn't have to hide my struggles from her. She was strict, but she knew what was going on in my head when I wouldn't raise my hand for fear that I would give a wrong answer.

A few minutes later Mrs. Miller sat on top of the desk across from me. "Jerry," she began, "we're about to start a school-wide unit about safety. Today the class will be given steps to follow in case of a fire, and here's where you can help. I've seen the drawings in your sketchpad. You have all kinds of vehicles in there, like airplanes and military tanks. Would you draw us something for fire prevention week? Maybe a fire engine? You can use your talents for extra credit. It will bring your grades up."

"Really? My drawing could help me with school?" I'd never imagined that. It seemed too good to be true.

"With your challenges, you'll need to work much harder than your classmates,"

she said. "But I truly believe you can become whatever you want to be. It's a pity we don't have more role models like Henry O. Tanner."

"Who is Henry O. Tanner?" I asked.

"He's a gifted Colored artist who has received much recognition. Mr. Tanner is a painter who studied right here in Philadelphia. Maybe," she added, "by the time you finish your schooling, more Colored artists will be recognized." In that moment I was especially glad my teacher looked like me, and that my parents had sent me to Hill Elementary.

Right then the recess bell rang, and within moments my classmates rushed in. Once everyone was seated, Mrs. Miller explained that we were starting a safety unit. "Next week there will be a short film in morning assembly titled *Duck and Cover*, about how to protect yourself in case of an atomic bomb, something you've probably heard about in the short news parade films at the cinema. But right now, it's time for us to go over our rules for a fire drill."

This time the butterflies in my stomach were from excitement. When Mrs. Miller got to the part about the fire department, I could hardly wait for her to call my name.

"Jerry is our class artist," she announced, and I stood right up. "He'll be drawing all of the parts of a fire engine for us."

On any other day I would have felt anxious to get up in front of the class, but not this time. I grabbed the chalk and quickly sketched out the wheels, the ladders, and the hose, eager to show that I wanted to participate and learn, even if it wasn't in the usual way. It made me feel good—and safe—inside and out.

I would hold on to this feeling and use it to work even harder on those areas that were so challenging for me. I wanted to learn, and now I had my own unique way: through drawing. The bridge to my understanding of an idea or subject was to draw it, and if there was nothing to draw on, I would sketch it out in my brain.

After that day, I would be called upon to draw anything that needed an illustrated explanation—and often, even things that didn't.

"Very good," Mrs. Miller would say, beaming. "That's just perfect."

CHAPTER 5

RUNNING THE STREETS

When we weren't in school or doing chores, my buddies and I turned East Earlham Street into our playground. Since there was no through traffic, we were free to play in the street. We created a much larger world in our imaginations than we actually had in the physical space of our small block.

The area under the fire escapes of the Blaisdell pencil factory became a place for me and my friends to play basketball; we used the space between the rungs of an extension ladder as our "net." The narrow alley that separated the factory from the row homes on East Earlham offered another favorite pastime: We'd climb that brick wall by putting our backs against it and our feet against the opposite building, using our hands and legs to shimmy up to the second-story roof.

I'd saved up some money from shining shoes on Germantown Avenue to buy a bow and arrow, which we used for target practice, but other than

that, we mostly used whatever was available to create things. Wheels from old skates and wooden crates discarded by stores were turned into a kind of scooter called a "skate-do," and discarded fences and other wooden junk became shoeshine boxes. When you made a one-of-a-kind thing, you had full ownership—a little something that no one else had.

The clubhouse we'd constructed was made of slats of old fence on three sides, with the fourth side being the stone wall of the vacant lot. The floor was made of red brick, since it wasn't hard to find castoffs from torn-down structures and old sidewalks. We were especially proud of the fact that the structure had one real glass window.

Five of us often met up at the clubhouse on weekends, trying to figure out what to do to pass the time. As much as we'd managed to expand our world on East Earlham, as we got older, it started to feel limited, and we were always craving adventure.

"What about riding down to Ben Franklin Bridge?" said Alfred late one afternoon. "We haven't done that for a while!"

"We'll have to be back before curfew," I reminded them. There had recently been gang activity in the city, and kids under the age of eighteen had to be indoors before dark.

"That's too far," nine-year-old Sonny chimed in. "Y'all know I can't go."

"You can ride with me until we get to Auggie's," I told him, since I was eleven now. "Hop on behind me."

"Let's go!" Bobby called out. Charging forward on our bikes, we weaved our way through our packed block, with Sonny stretching his legs on either side of me.

East Earlham Street was like an open-air market, playground, and place for folks to hang out on building stoops, trying to beat the heat. We swerved around Miss Sadie as she waited in line to buy fresh vegetables; Moe the Ice Man, with a dripping block of ice slung over his

shoulder; my sisters, playing jacks with their friends; and Uncle Alec, swapping stories with the menfolk about his latest cross-country haul of iceboxes. The spirit of Southern storytelling was very much a part of how my neighbors communicated: animated, with a lot of drama and a little bit of stretching the truth.

At Auggie's grocery, I made a suggestion. "Let's pick up some soda pops now. We won't be able to buy any downtown," I reminded my friends. Downtown, we never really knew which stores would serve us. It always felt like a risk to walk in anywhere.

Quickly we gulped down Cokes and got back on our bikes. "See you guys when you come back," Sonny mumbled, and walked glumly back toward our familiar dead-end street.

We moved mostly as a pack when venturing beyond East Earlham. You couldn't really call us a gang, though—not like the Tioga Ts or the other territorial gangs surrounding Germantown. We didn't have any name or colors, there were no initiation rites, and there were too few of us. We were just the boys from East Earlham Street, good friends.

We rode through neighborhoods we never could have lived in, or imagined living in, past stores that we were not allowed to enter. As we rode up Coulter Street and then made our way across the trolley tracks on Germantown Avenue, it was hard not to notice how the neighborhoods

changed. The houses got bigger and bigger, with front yards, flowering bushes, and walkways leading to wide porches with wicker furniture. Here we saw few people, and even fewer cars parked on the street. It felt like another world. There were no hucksters, no kids on go-carts or roller skates, and no sounds except for me and my buddies bantering with one another.

The houses looked more familiar to me when we reached Midvale Avenue, where some of Dad's customers lived. Sometimes he let me tag along to his job sites, carrying paint cans, brushes, and drop cloths. Dad always had a weighty ring of a dozen or more keys attached to his overalls, one for each customer. If no one was home, he was able to let himself in to work. That was

how much Dad had earned his customers' respect, and it was how I began to recognize the value of being trustworthy. Funny that he spent so much time fixing up white people's fancy homes, but hardly ever did anything like that at our house. That was just the way it was.

Bobby pulled ahead of the group as the leader, whistling as loud as he could, making certain that we didn't bike through any neighborhoods where there were gang turfs. As we reached the top of a steep in-cline, I let my feet slide off the pedals and coasted all the way down to the road that runs alongside the Schuylkill River. With a burst of energy, we started joking around, unaware of the cars whizzing by on the wide roadway, barely noticing the bright flags of differ-ent countries and grassy concrete islands separating many lanes of traffic.

As we approached the Benjamin Franklin Bridge, the ramp sloped upward, and my legs pumped harder as we neared its mid-dle. We always stopped at the highest point and leaned our bikes

against the guardrails, taking in the awesome sight of the sun reflecting on the Delaware River. Here was one of the few places away from East Earlham Street where we didn't feel unwelcome. The knots I often felt in my stomach and the tightening in my chest could relax here.

It was impossible for us to hear one another. The piercing sound of

blaring car horns and tractor trailers cut through the constant drone of engines speeding by and the *thump, thump, thump* of tires on the road's surface. Much like East Earlham Street, there was constant movement in the river, since both sides were lined with shipping ports. But unlike on East Earlham, everything here appeared to be moving in slow

motion—sailboats, cargo ships, and barges—which meant it created the perfect opportunity for me to draw.

I took my sketchpad out of my bike basket and feverishly began sketching a tugboat before it passed under the bridge and disappeared. It never really mattered much to me what I was drawing. It was the drawing itself that mattered.

When Elsworth began waving his arms and pointing back toward home, I pretended not to understand. The signal to split always seemed to happen before I was ready to leave. I hated being pulled away in the middle of a drawing.

As the boys mounted their bikes, Bobby coasted over and signaled for my sketchbook. Motioning to Elsworth and Alfred, he showed them the tugboat, giving a thumbs-up. It made me happy that my friends

appreciated my art—even though sometimes my passion for drawing meant I spent less time with them.

"It's not finished yet," I called out as we began pedaling urgently down the pedestrian lane to reach East Earlham Street before curfew. But every now and then we let go of the handlebars and pedaled hands-free, with outstretched arms over our heads.

Just then Bobby decided to pull ahead as the leader again, flashing a wide smile, feeling free and in charge. But then we turned a corner, and suddenly he shouted, "Red car!"

The clowning stopped instantly. Our anxious eyes stared straight ahead, and my heart thudded loudly in my chest, even though we weren't doing anything wrong.

I was very aware of the unjust attitude of some people that Blacks could not be trusted. Knowing that we were frowned upon by this other side of Philly usually made us turn and run in the opposite direction when we spotted the fire engine–red police cars that patrolled our streets. Even in broad daylight, we panicked at the sight of them, instinctively feeling that the cops were suspect, instead of people to be looked to for help.

The car slowed as it passed in the opposite direction. My grip tightened on the handlebars as I looked back over my shoulder.

"Aw, no!" I called out. "They're turning around!"

With flashing lights, the vehicle slowly followed us. It took all my self-control not to pedal faster as it pulled alongside us. We could feel the cops staring.

Then, just as suddenly as it had appeared, the red car sped away. But seeing the cops was a reminder of what Dad had told me over and over: "If you ever get picked up by the police, cooperate and tell the truth—don't lie!"

There was no chance that I'd ever lie to a cop, but there was always a chance we boys could get picked up by the police for no reason at all. It just wasn't fair.

"Jerry," Bobby called back to me after

the car was out of sight, "bet you were scared, weren't you?"

"Naw, man…heck no!" I answered, faking a smile as wide as his, my heart still pounding. When the top of the next hill was in sight, I stood up and bore down on the pedals with all the strength I could muster.

By the time we reached East Earlham Street, the sky was a deep, dark blue, but we'd made it there before curfew. I scrambled up the stoop.

Inside, I found Claudia and Helen in the living room, huddled in front of the black-and-white television, and Joan was slouched in Mother's chair. Usually, seeing Mother quietly reading in that chair meant all was well with the world. I missed seeing her there right now.

"You missed dinner," Claudia said, rolling her eyes.

"Boy, are you in trouble!" Joan said with her usual scowl, not realizing how close I'd come to being in *real* trouble with the cops.

I went into the kitchen and gobbled down every bit of the ham, string beans, mashed potatoes, and corn bread that Mother had left for me on a plate covered by another upside-down plate. She'd set it over a pot of water on a low flame to keep the food warm.

After I ate, I washed my dishes and placed them in the rack to dry.

"I'm home," I called up to Mother, climbing the stairs.

"Did you eat?" Mother asked. "Everything washed and put away?"

"Yes, Mother," I said, reversing direction as quietly as I could. I had to remember to be trustworthy, always.

Back in the kitchen I dried the dishes and utensils, then silently placed them in the cabinet. As soon as that was done, I tiptoed up to my room and completed my sketch of the tugboat. Each stroke took me back to the best part of the day: Bobby's thumbs-up, watching the tugboat as it disappeared beneath us, with that feeling of being free to go anywhere.

Before the cops came along and reminded me that I wasn't.

CHAPTER 6

UNDER THE PIER

It was summertime, and my family and I, along with my friend Sonny, had packed ourselves into my Dad's Ford Woodie station wagon and crossed the Benjamin Franklin Bridge to drive to the Jersey Shore. Whenever we stopped for a light or a stop sign, people could not help but stare at the car's deep green hood and fenders, chrome bumpers and hubcaps. When it was clean and polished, boy, the wood grain of the dark brown and honey–colored cab caught everyone's eye. Being the first family on East Earlham Street to own a car, it made us feel really proud.

On these trips my parents usually rented the same apartment on Missouri Avenue, in the segregated section of Atlantic City, which was where the Black families stayed. From

the second-floor balcony, Sonny and I loved to watch folks parading every which way, pouring in and out of restaurants, dressed up and strutting to the jukebox music drifting out of nightclubs and bars all day long.

"Come on, boys," Joan called one morning. "It's time to head for the boardwalk."

Sonny and I, wearing bathing trunks under our khakis, grabbed towels and ran downstairs to join my three sisters and my parents. (By this time, Billy and Eddie were both away in the service.)

Off we all went, carrying blankets, a basket of food, and a large Thermos. "Keep your eyes open," Dad had directed us before leaving the apartment. "You never know who you might see." Once, Uncle Alec told Dad that he almost bumped into "the Brown Bomber"—the boxer Joe Louis—and that he had also spotted the world-famous performer Sammy Davis Jr.

With anticipation we crossed over the boardwalk, weaving our way through vendors, shoppers, passenger carts, and little kids tagging alongside parents. At the bottom of the stairs to the sandy shore we stepped onto the Black section known as Chicken Bone Beach. This area wasn't regularly cleaned and cared for like the white beach. The sand was grayish in color, unlike the bright bone-colored sand where white people spread their blankets and ate their lunches.

But everyone was still enjoying their time in the sun. Animated voices filled the air, people in conversation as if just leaving church or enjoying a chance meeting on a street corner, sharing bright smiles, warm hugs, and so many stories. Men in long pants and Stetson hats sporting

blazers, ladies with flowing dresses and fancy bonnets, and brown bodies in bathing suits were clustered on both sides of the wooden walkway.

"Let's race to the water, Sonny," I suggested as soon as we'd found a spot for our beach blankets among a crowd of sunbathers on wooden folding chairs. Both of us slipped out of our clothes and took off for the ocean's edge, dodging crashing waves. It wasn't just the ocean we stepped into, but a sea of Black life, as well.

I wasn't a good swimmer, but I waded in up to my chest and hoisted Sonny onto my shoulders any-way. He couldn't swim much, either, but he dove right into the shallows, returning to the surface coughing up salt water. Eventually we headed back to the beach, then cartwheeled over to our blankets.

"You boys cut that foolishness out," said Mother. "Can't you see how much sand you're kicking up over folks? Take your nonsense underneath the boardwalk. Go look for your cousins."

We found Cousin Herbie and the other boys under the pier. The two beaches were separated by Steel Pier, which was for white people only. Built of wood and metal, it jutted far out into the ocean on stilts and was the hub of the boardwalk, with penny arcades and the clang of coin-operated games that offered the chance to win a stuffed animal. Square towers rose up two stories high, and there was a large structure mounted with lamps to bring light to big events.

Steel Pier was also the place to find the world-famous diving horse.

I would read the posters announcing the times and ticket prices for the performances, but I knew there were no entry tickets for those of us on the Black side. Instead, I'd walk close to the boardwalk and listen to the loud chatter of an eager crowd, the announcer's excited voice booming into a microphone as the horse and its rider approached the edge of the elevated platform. I'd shield my eyes from the glare of the brilliant sun and look in the direction of the sounds, but I couldn't see anything from where I stood.

Instead of hanging out on the pier, my cousins and I played underneath it. Using its support pilings as bases, we chased, tackled, and wrestled one another in game after game.

"What about dodgeball?" I suggested this time. It was a game I loved because I was fast, small, and hard to hit. Herbie, the tallest of the boys, quickly shot the ball at me. I ducked as it whizzed over my head, bouncing farther under the pier, where I followed it.

Sounds of stomping feet and raucous voices boomed above our heads. For a moment I was lost in the noise of fun and excitement, until

Herbie yelled, "Who's going after the ball, some slowpoke?" Then came another zinger: "I think it's *Shorty*!"

His words rang in my ears. Quickly I tossed the ball back and dashed out into the bright sunlight, blinking as my eyes adjusted from the deep shadows under the pier.

"Folks are cheering on the pier," I blurted. "Let's go check it out."

How I envied those white children, so close to the action, whose hearts would pound as they witnessed the horse and its rider dive hundreds of feet to plunge into a tank of water. I could hear the splash, and I'd imagine feeling the water's spray as the pair disappeared and reappeared again, the rider's hands raised in triumph.

"I'm not going!" Sonny snapped. "You know they won't let us in."

"I just want to see what all the screaming is about," I told him, even though I knew perfectly well. "You can stay here, Scaredy Cat!" I called to him, skipping stairs on my way up to the pier.

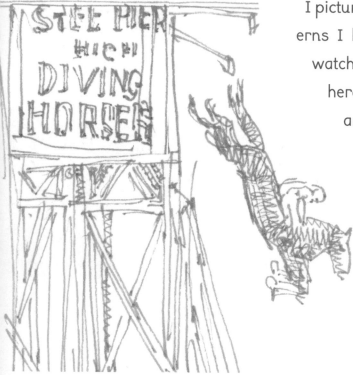

I pictured the cowboys from the Westerns I had spent countless Saturdays watching as a younger boy. After herding cattle, breaking wild horses, and maybe a gunfight or two, the cowboys always ended up running from some threat. Horse and rider would plunge into a river—maybe the Rio Grande or the Snake River—and emerge on the other side, victorious and safe. *Was it anything like that?* I wondered.

My heart thumped faster and faster as I inched toward the pier's entrance with its gigantic poster: STEEL PIER HIGH-DIVING HORSES. SHOWPLACE OF THE NATION.

Right then—cutting through the sounds of a blaring loudspeaker, organ music, pinball machines, and the noisy crowd—I heard my name called out sharply.

"Jerry!"

Before I knew it, Dad had come up from behind and spun me around. Without saying another word, he walked me back to Chicken Bone Beach. I shrank down close to Mother.

Dad's mouth tightened. "Talk to your son!" he said, then walked away.

Mother looked into my eyes. "We have more than enough right here among our own folks," she said, "not to want what white people deny us. Jim and I have worked hard, Jerry, and we're proud that we can provide all that is needed for our family."

There was no question we had the tastiest, most mouth-watering comfort food; the best toe-tapping, head-shaking, soul-stirring music; the most animated laughter; the tightest hugs of friends meeting friends. But we did not have the magic of the diving horse.

Like the balls bouncing around in the pinball machines on the pier, my feelings ricocheted from the upset of Dad being sore with me to the comfort of Mother's words, even though I didn't fully understand them. She always talked about "having enough." Why didn't she want more?

Mother patted my hand. "Jerry, Jim's not angry with you. He fears that someday you might be in a situation where he can't protect you. I worry, too." She sighed, then changed the subject. "Are you boys hungry?"

As she pulled some fried chicken and potato salad out of her basket, deep inside I knew that Mother was right about having enough. But still, I could only imagine what it would be like to see the horse and rider the way they were shown on the poster. Not even Mother could wash away my upset that Black people weren't allowed to attend the show.

Sonny was watching us from under the pier. "Sonny," Mother called, "come and get something to eat."

I said nothing to him during lunch, angry that he had tattled on me. Sonny ate silently, staring at the ocean. Afterward he went back to play with my cousins.

I closed my eyes, imagining what the diving horse and rider would look like. Then I began sketching. The splash was the hardest part to draw.

The hommes on the ...

remem...

...draw...

...

so...

...

...d s... beer bottles and the *use*

...nber well the color amb. *deen r...*

Meeting John L.

to the alleyway where we would
se the alley of the first *house*
and ...

PART 3

OUT IN THE WORLD

CHAPTER 7

IN THE COUNTRY

Growing up in Philadelphia, I was a city kid through and through. But when my Aunt Helen and Uncle Osbie bought a piece of land in Berlin, New Jersey, I found out I loved the countryside, too. My dad and uncles were helping to build their house, so we had lots of excuses to go visit that summer.

"Colored folks buying land and building their own house, that's a big deal! Ain't that something!" my Aunt Jenny had said. For me, going to New Jersey was more like going to another country, not just the state next door. And the Delaware River wasn't like a river at all; it seemed like an ocean.

Dad seemed to know everything about building: laying foundations, putting up cinder–block walls, carpentry, electricity, you name it! Uncle Osbie had put him in charge, so he was eager to get to New Jersey early on this particular Labor Day weekend and get to work.

"The interior should be done by late fall," Dad told Mother. "Osbie and Helen should be able to move in before winter sets in."

Our family was the first to arrive. Aunt Jenny and Uncle Harold came next, with their four children—Connie, Fannie, Herbie, and Pee Wee—piled in their Buick. Aunt Julia and Uncle Fred were right behind them. As on other weekends, car after car pulled into the sandy driveway with horns honking. Children's hands and heads poked out of windows, waving and calling to cousins, even before their cars had come to

complete stops. Everybody poured out of doors, in a hurry to hug, shake hands, and swap greetings like they hadn't seen one another in years. In fact, most of us had been there the week before.

Labor Day was on the upcoming Monday, so the men would have an extra day to work on the house. But since it was a holiday weekend, a barbeque was planned for Labor Day. Preparations began almost immediately as Mother and my aunts moved off toward the kitchen,

chattering all at once, their conversations almost blending into song. My uncles unloaded the cars, and the girl cousins disappeared together.

Most of the male cousins and their friends gathered in a huddle, including my friend Bobby, who had come with us. I hung back, not sure that I wanted to be a part of whatever they were up to. These boys were mostly older than I was, and they played rough. I remembered the last time we had visited. My cousins loved arm wrestling and pretend fight-

ing, and they had marked off a square in the sand for a boxing ring. I was paired up with a bigger kid with a teasing grin. I knew how to protect myself, since I had taken boxing lessons at the Police Athletic League in Philly, so I went along with the game, dodging the boy's punches. Still, it wasn't much fun to go up against someone who was so much stronger than I was.

I wondered if I should get out my bow and arrow, which might impress them, but thought better of it. These boys might break it, and it was my prized possession.

Just then Cousin Herbie pulled me aside. "We're going to swim in the quarry," he whispered excitedly.

I hesitated. I didn't know how to swim well, and Aunt Helen had warned us: "Don't go there, it's too dangerous. No one knows how deep it is. Someone could drown!" But since all of the boys had agreed to go, I nodded. Even though I was the fastest runner, I lagged behind the group tearing off to the quarry.

When we reached the quarry rim, T-shirts and pants were flung off. Shoes and sneakers were piled high upon rocks. Because we were surrounded by knotted pines, tangled vines, and weeds, no one could see us half-naked boys in our underwear.

"Last one in is a rotten egg!" Herbie called. Immediately the sound of bodies breaking the surface of the water rippled across the quarry. I froze as panic took hold of me. The boys seemed to stay underwater for too long.

After what seemed like an eternity, Bobby and my cousins finally bounded out of the water on the far side. Within moments of spotting me, they circled back around the quarry and grabbed my arms and ankles. Then, with a wide swing, they tossed me in.

"Now you'll have to learn how to swim!" yelled Pee Wee.

At first all I saw was blue sky. Then I hit the water and went under, and everything turned a muddy brown, the color of the rocky walls.

A gargling sound filled my ears, and I flailed my arms and legs, struggling to get my head above the water. When I broke the surface, I took a deep breath, but I inhaled more water than air. I coughed fiercely and splashed wildly, pretty sure I was going to die.

I did manage to make it to the water's edge, but it was more thrashing than swimming—like a scene in one of those adventure movies, where the hero gets caught in quicksand. Well, I sure didn't feel like much of a hero as I clawed my way out, especially since I could hear the other boys snickering behind me.

Holding on to my wet boxer shorts so they wouldn't fall off, I worked up a smile and gave a thumbs-up, as if I were victorious.

Quickly gathering my things, I called out, "Need to get back. Just remem—bered something I'm supposed to do for my ol' man." I scrambled away as fast as I could, only stopping long enough to put my clothes on.

Once I'd escaped, I just wanted to be alone. I went to our car to get my bow and quiver and headed deep into the woods. "Who cares about swimming, anyway?" I mumbled.

Unlike on East Earlham Street, there were no chaotic sounds in the forest. Chattering squirrels, bird calls, and my own footsteps were all I could hear as I walked among pine trees, tangled brush, and tall grasses. Here I didn't have to pretend to be anything. No trying to read, no trying to spell, no feeling stupid, no looking for Dad's approval, and no friends or cousins making me do something I didn't want to do. I felt as if I belonged.

As I splashed across a shallow stream, I startled a flock of wild turkeys. Their flight sounded like helicopters. At my feet among the green and straw-colored underbrush lay a single feather, which reminded me of those sometimes worn by Native people in movies I had seen. I slipped it into my quiver alongside the arrows, imagining myself to be a powerful hunter. Had Native people once lived on this land where my aunt and uncle's house was being built?

Scanning the trees, I entered a clearing and spotted a bird perched on the branch of a dwarf pine tree. I took out an arrow, loaded the bow, raised it up, and let it fly.

My heart jumped into my throat as the bird fell silently to the ground. There may have been no sound in the forest, but the roar in my head seemed deafening.

"Oh, no!" I cried, never thinking my arrow would hit a target. With palms sweating and a wave of nausea washing over me, I hesitantly approached the bird.

What should I do? Should I leave it here? I wondered as I inched closer. Anxiously I picked up the arrow and the bird's limp, warm body.

I was relieved, for a short moment, that there was no blood. But the force of my arrow had accidentally ended the bird's life.

I groaned in despair.

Mother will know what I should do. I'll take it to her.

My head hanging low, I headed toward the house. The pounding of my heart seemed even louder than the sawing of wood in the distance. Before long, I spotted Mother's yellow sunbonnet. She was carrying a bucket and a shovel, on her way back from digging up sassafras roots for brewing tea. I tried not to look sad as I approached her.

"Why so gloomy, Jerry?" Mother knew me too well. "And…what are you holding behind your back?" I couldn't hide anything from her.

"Mother," I blurted, staring at the ground. "I messed up. I killed a bird. I didn't mean to, but it happened. I shot it with my bow and arrow."

Mother gently lifted my chin. "It was an accident, right?"

"Yes. I didn't mean to do it. If only I hadn't...!"

"Hush, Jerry," whispered Mother. "Nobody has to know about this but you, me, and the Lord, who has already forgiven you. Come on now," she said softly. "Hand it here. We'll bury it." She took me to the base of the tree where she had been digging. I walked beside her, dragging my bow and quiver through the dirt.

Mother wrapped the bird in leaves and placed it in a hole. With trembling hands, I covered it with sand, then placed a small rock on top to mark the grave.

Saturday afternoon and evening were a seesaw of emotional ups and downs. Dancing on the patio with Joan's 45 rpm rhythm–and–blues records on the turn-table until dusk was an "up." Joking with the guys as we gathered wood to be used in the roasting pit for Monday was fun. And Aunt Julia's potato salad, fresh picked vegetables, and Mother's coconut cake were other high points.

But thoughts of the bird would not leave my mind. That night, the men and boys laid sleeping bags outside. As I tried to fall asleep, I listened to the night sounds of a great horned owl, katydids, field crickets, and tree frogs. Just when I finally drifted off, Uncle Osbie's prize rooster started crowing, the sounds of chattering birds filled the morning air, and sunshine came through the trees.

On the day of the barbeque, we were up at daybreak, helping to prepare the pit for the cookout, until the slaughtered and dressed pig was roasting slowly over burning coals.

"Boys," said Uncle Osbie, "you all pay close attention to the pit. Keep turning those coals. Add more wood when needed. And don't let the fire go out!"

"Osbie!" Aunt Helen called from inside. "Goodness mercy, the electricity is out, and we're all out of fuses! Maybe you can borrow some from one of the neighbors—the hardware stores are closed today."

Then she called me and Pee Wee over to her. "My newborn chicks were being kept warm by electric lights strung through the crawl space under the house. You two are small enough to shimmy on your backs and hand out the chicks. If something isn't done right away, they could die!"

Pee Wee and I felt really important. Suddenly I realized that being small wasn't such a bad thing.

"Now, you boys take care handling my chicks," she said. "And be careful of the bulbs! They may still be hot."

"Come on, Pee Wee," I said. "Let's be real quiet so we don't scare them."

Silently we crawled through dark shadows toward the peeping chicks. Holding a new life in the palm of my hand, hearing its little *peeps*, and feeling the frightened bird's heart beating brought Mother's words back: *You are forgiven.*

One by one, we gently handed the baby chicks out to the other boys. Then they placed them in the sun on beds of straw that Aunt Helen had fixed in fruit crates. Helping save these tiny lives seemed like the most important job in the world.

"There! That'll be fine until we're able to get the electricity back on," Aunt Helen reassured us. When it was all done, Pee Wee and I were hot and sweaty from crawling among the eggshells in the crawl space.

"Come on," I said, "let's get washed."

"Race you to the pump," he responded. We took turns pumping with our hands cupped, trying to clean our faces in the cold water before it slipped through our fingers.

Before long, it seemed like it was time for everybody to get cleaned up for Monday's holiday supper of roasted pig, potato salad, corn on the cob, string beans, yeast rolls, watermelon slices, and Mother's peach cobbler for dessert.

"Jerry!" Bobby headed over to me while gobbling down some food.

"You should have stayed with us yesterday. You missed all the fun. Did you help your dad?"

"Yeah!" I lied, without hesitating. All the other boys were laughing and whispering together with lowered voices, so the grown-ups couldn't hear about their adventures.

Feeling left out, I went to get my sketchpad from our car, then went behind the house. With my back leaning against the cinder-block foundation, I sharpened a pencil with my penknife and began drawing the bird from the forest, its wings spread wide, ready to fly away and take care of its own chicks.

Right then Mother peered around the corner. "There you are," she said softly. In her hands was a slice of cake. "You didn't eat much of your food—even the ribs, the chicken, or your favorite dessert."

"I didn't feel much like eating, Mother." I scribbled more lines on my drawing, but the bird still didn't look alive enough.

"I should have known, Jerry," she responded. "I understand."

CHAPTER 8

WORKING THE NEWSSTAND

The following year, summer went by in a flash. Hot and sticky Philly rolled into September and Labor Day, our last summer celebration with family at Aunt Helen and Uncle Osbie's. Butterflies fluttered in my stomach because I was entering the eighth grade and starting a new school, Theodore Roosevelt Junior High, one year after most of the other students, who hadn't come from Hill Elementary.

Roosevelt had both Black and white students, and most of my classmates had already formed tight friendships. None of my friends from the block were there, but Vinny Pugliese and I hit it off right away, even though Black and white students

at Roosevelt didn't hang out with one another. It was an unwritten code.

At the beginning of eighth grade, I was almost thirteen. Since at the time young people in Philadelphia could have part-time jobs starting at age thirteen, I was thinking more about how to earn money to help the family. For years, the guys from the block and I had been earning pocket change shining shoes in front of the Woolworth five-and-dime store. We'd wait near the entrance, hoping that men leaving the store would want a

fifteen–cent shoeshine. Man, I was good at it. But fifteen cents a shine didn't add up to much, especially when I was sharing it with the household.

Around then I noticed that there were newsstands on all four corners of Germantown and Chelten Avenues, but that the stand on Chelten Avenue in front of Rowell's department store was shuttered and padlocked. On most days, people crowded around the three open stands, especially when a bus or trolley opened its doors and the passengers spilled out. I

saw an opportunity on that unattended street corner.

One day, I hesitantly approached the tall white man wearing horn–rimmed glasses selling newspapers at one of the larger stands. I'd noticed that he always seemed to have an ear–to–ear smile. Strapped around his waist was a money changer, as well as a half apron with deep pockets. He looked at me over the rim of his glasses.

"Are you the boss?" I asked.

"Sure enough," he responded, grinning wide, as he often did. "What's up?"

"I'm looking for work," I told him.

"Ever sell newspapers?"

"No, sir, but I can learn."

"Well," he said, "I'll need you

promptly on Mondays to Fridays from three to six, and Saturdays from twelve to six. The pay is six dollars a week. I've hired other boys, and it didn't work."

"I'm used to work. I help my dad." While he waited on customers, I nervously continued to ramble on about everything I'd done with Dad and how reliable I was.

He must have gotten tired of listening to me because he finally agreed. "Can you start next week? My name is Matt Schainberg. What's yours?"

"I'm Jerry Pinkney. Thanks for the job, Mr. Matt."

He took off his glasses and gave me a puzzled expression. "I know the name Pinkney from somewhere. Can't remember right now. Monday, three PM sharp," he added, "and call me Matt."

"Sure, Matt!" I ran excitedly across Germantown Avenue, looking at the shuttered hood of the newsstand with PHILADELPHIA BULLETIN stenciled across it.

I've got a job! And I'm sure glad he never asked me how old I am! I thought. I could hardly wait to tell Mother and Dad.

That Monday my anticipation about the new job outweighed my anxiety about going to Roosevelt, where I had to hide my trouble with reading from a whole new set of teachers. It was such hard work just to be *okay*; there was so much energy and pain and exhaustion spent to cover up my sense of failure, to try not to be seen only in terms of my learning disability. It was like leading a double life.

But the day went by in a blur, and after school ended at 2:15, Vinny and I met up a block away from school, where we wouldn't be noticed by other kids. We usually walked home together, since his Italian neighborhood was in the same direction as East Earlham Street.

"Just got a job selling newspapers," I blurted, "at the corner of Germantown and Chelten. Need to be there by three. Gotta hurry. See you tomorrow!"

"I used to deliver papers on my bike!" Vinny called as I took off running.

When I arrived, it was 2:45 and I was out of breath. The padlock had been removed from the stand where I would soon be working, and the hood was up. Matt was arranging magazines.

"Matt," I announced, "I'm here!"

"Early, huh?" he responded. "Buckle this money changer around your waist. Here's how it works. The paper costs a nickel, but your customers will not always have the exact amount. Oftentimes you'll need to make change. Let's say someone pays with a quarter. Put it in the slot marked 'twenty-five.' Then push twice on the dime lever."

"Got it," I said.

"Today you start off with twenty papers,"

said Matt. "Come back for more if needed. Mondays are always slow. Can't figure that out, since news is always happening."

I made my way back across the street, this time taking it slow to be sure I didn't trip on the raised trolley tracks or the uneven cobblestones. I didn't want to drop the papers.

For the next couple of hours, every time a trolley or bus pulled up, I yelled, "Get your dailies here!" With a *Bulletin* and a *Daily News* at arm's length, I made sure that those headlines and pictures could be seen. "Come get your dailies!" I barked.

But eventually my voice got hoarse, and very few of my papers had sold. Most people kept on walking as if they didn't see or hear me, or they crossed the street to one of the other stands.

I had a back-and-forth conversation with myself. *Am I someplace I shouldn't be?* I wondered. *If I weren't Colored, would they buy my papers? But Matt hired me. He's white. And he thinks I can sell papers.*

I wasn't sure what to think. Feeling out of place was weighing heavily on me. Mother had often told us, "If you don't know you are going to be welcomed somewhere, leave." Trying to sell these papers to white folks felt like staring in the window of a store where I wasn't sure what would happen if I went inside.

Right then I spotted a welcome distraction from my doubts and worries: Burton's Paint Store, on the other side of Chelten Avenue. I had been there with Dad before, when he was buying paint, brushes, and wallpaper. Each time, I'd been transfixed by

the array of jars, paint tubes, and boxes of pastels. Their art supplies section held an endless assortment of drawing pads, much bigger than the sketchbooks Dad had bought for me, and a huge display of brushes, all shapes and sizes, fat and skinny. I was spellbound. I couldn't imagine what an artist would do with so many different tools and materials. But I wanted to find out.

I wished I could have my sketchbook with me to pass the time when there were no customers. But would I even dare? I was hired to sell papers, after all.

Monday ended with me returning my unsold newspapers. "It's only your first day," said Matt. "Remember, Jerry, Mondays are always slow." Disappointed, I trudged home.

"How was school today?" Mother asked as soon as the screen door slammed behind me.

"Okay," I replied. Then she asked about the newsstand. I gave the same answer. "Got homework," I said, then ran up to my room.

On Tuesday, Wednesday, and Thursday I still couldn't sell my allotment of papers. On Friday, as quitting time approached, I took a quarter from my pocket that I had earned shining shoes, placed it into its chamber in my money changer, and looked around, then folded up five papers and took them to a nearby trash can. With my back toward Matt, I made sure all of them were covered up, then went back to my stand and called, "Get your dailies here!"

I couldn't stand the idea of disappointing Matt. I cared about being a good worker. Because of my poor reading and spelling, I felt like I had to

make up for it by being excellent at everything else—like being respon-
sible, dependable, and prompt.

My thoughts of disappointment were interrupted by a familiar voice.

"How ya doing, favorite nephew?" Aunt Edna had just walked up to
me with a proud grin on her face.

Before I could answer, she went on, "I just spoke with Matt, and he's
pleased with how hard you're working. He says that you shouldn't get
discouraged. Sales will pick up in time. Hand me one of those *Bulletin*s,
and a *Daily News* as well," she said, handing me a dime. "Here you go,
young man. I can't wait to tell that brother of mine who I
bought my paper from today!"

That afternoon I walked home feeling guilty about the papers I'd put in the trash. *It's not like I lied*, I told myself. *But what can I do to sell more papers and make it up to Matt?*

Saturday was a crowded day on the avenue. I had three papers left, and it was six o'clock. I decided to stay, determined to sell out. At ten past six I headed for Matt's stand, grinning, with my palms up. "All sold out!"

Matt laughed as he reached into his apron. It was payday. One by one he counted out six one-dollar bills. "What do you plan to do with your money?"

"Half goes to Mother to help out with bills and stuff." This was the way it worked in our house, when any of us got a job. "I'm not sure about the three dollars I have left. There's a large drawing pad in Burton's, but I don't know if I have enough."

"Now I remember!" exclaimed Matt. "Edna Pinkney told me about her talented nephew who loves to draw. That's *you*! Whenever she's in the neighborhood she stops here for papers. Your Aunt Edna sure loves to talk."

"You mean she talked to you about me?"

"Yep! She told me that you graduated from Hill School with some kind of achievement award for being the top male student!" That was true—even after all my difficulties, the teachers at Hill had rewarded me with a shiny medal for how much effort I'd put into overcoming my reading challenges. It wasn't until many years later that I came to understand that I had a condition called dyslexia.

After my conversation with Matt, I whistled all the way home, feeling satisfied about my first pay—day and the things Aunt Edna had said. I could hardly wait to find out if I had enough to buy that big sketchpad.

"How's that new job?" Miss Sadie called out from her front window.

"Sold out of papers!" I told her in a hurry, eager to get home and tell Mother.

"I got paid, Mother!" I called as I walked in, making sure the screen door didn't slam. "I made six dollars," I added, handing her three.

Mother tucked the bills into her apron pocket and hugged me. I went off to my room, listening to Mother humming "Precious Lord, Take My Hand."

On Monday, I left school in a hurry to get to Burton's, and I went straight to the art supply aisle. In a mad rush I knocked over a display of drawing pencils and quickly gathered them up. I didn't want to be late for the newsstand.

With shaky hands I grabbed a sketchpad and a pencil, then headed to the checkout counter. Mr. Allen smiled when I approached. "Jim's not with you today, Jerry? Not used to seeing you without your dad. Should I put these things on Jim's account?"

"Not this time," I said. "I got three dollars of my own. Sorry about your pencils, Mr. Allen. I was too much in a hurry. I got myself a job right up the block. Mr. Matt hired me to sell newspapers."

"Since you're Jim's son," he responded, "I believe Matt's finally got someone he can depend on." Holding my breath, I waited while he checked the prices. "Jerry, you have enough for the sketchpad with some change, and the pencil is on me. On your way out, pick up another one! What time are you expected at the newsstand?"

"Now!" I said, looking up at the clock.

"My regards to your dad," Mr. Allen called as I ran out the door. "He always says, 'My son can really draw!'"

My heart skipped a beat.

As I headed to the newsstand, Mr. Allen's words ran through my head over and over. I felt a bit lighter and less anxious about being late. *Dad really told him that I could draw?* It was so hard to imagine Dad talking about my drawing like that.

"Bought that pad I told you about," I told Matt when I arrived.

Matt counted out my papers. "Here, Jerry. I won't start you off with as many today, but since it's Monday and you have that new sketchpad, I won't mind if you draw when the avenue is quiet. Just as long as you do your best to sell newspapers."

I couldn't believe my luck—getting to draw on the job!

Back at the stand, I slid my papers over to make room for the sketch-pad as I waited for people to get off the buses and trolleys. As I looked around for the next customer, I was trying to find things to draw as well. It turned out the perfect still life was right in front of me.

The headless mannequins in the Rowell's display window were dressed in sequined wedding gowns made of lace, with fancy embroidered flowers and decorative leaves. I opened my sketchpad. *These mannequins are perfect models.*

CHAPTER 9

ENTERING THE STUDIO

October began with an increase in the number of my customers. When there was a lull, I worked on sketchpad drawings, steadily penciling in the folds and patterns of decorative wedding gowns. Sometimes my buddies would snicker and tease me when they saw those drawings. But I didn't care. Now there was no more counting minutes until quitting time.

When there were no new displays in the Rowell's window to hold my attention, I began sketching people gazing at the gowned figures on the other side of the glass. It wasn't long before a customer spotted me.

"What are you working on?" she asked.

Turning my pad around, I said, "Just drawing."

"How about a *Bulletin* and a drawing?" she asked. I could hardly believe what she was asking.

"But it really doesn't look like you," I replied. "It's just a sketch. It could be better."

"It's a good drawing," she responded. "I like it. May I buy it? How much?"

"A nickel," I said, without thinking. "The same as a paper." I didn't have any idea what my drawing was worth. It was a shot in the dark. The paper was the only reference point I had. I felt a rush of pleasure and pride as she handed me the money for my drawing. Her nickel felt like gold.

It wasn't long before I was selling newspapers *and* drawings. So much so that one day when a customer wanted to buy a drawing of an elaborate bridal gown that I had worked on for days, I responded, "Sorry. Still working on it," without any intention of selling it. Now I could even pick and choose which drawings I wanted to sell.

I always remained watchful for regular customers, snapping to attention when they appeared. "Here you go," I'd say, handing them their paper and making change, then quickly going back to drawing. Occasionally I was so absorbed in a sketch that I didn't see a customer patiently waiting. Scrambling to appear alert, I would glance over to see if Matt was watching. There was no furrowed brow, just his usual smile.

On one of those days when I was lost in a drawing, I suddenly had a feeling that someone else was watching me. Looking up, I saw a man straining to see what I was working on.

"A *Bulletin* and *Daily News*," he requested.

"Sure," I responded. I recognized his face as someone I had seen in Burton's and talking to Matt.

"It's fun, watching you sketch. Matt tells me you're quite the drawer. May I see what else you have there?" he said, pointing to my sketchpad.

Slowly he turned each page, his expression both serious and pleased.

"I'm an artist, too," he said, opening a newspaper to the comics section. "My name is John Liney." He pointed to a row of panels with block letters that read HENRY. "I draw that comic strip," he announced.

"Wow!" I said. I could hardly believe I was talking to a *real* artist.

"My studio is right up the street, past Matt's newsstand. By the way, your boss is a close friend of mine. I always get my papers from Matt, and he told me about your drawings. Perhaps you'd like to see me at work tomorrow in my studio."

Right away I heard myself say, "Sure, Mr. Liney!"

"Come at ten of three," he said. "I'll speak to Matt. I'm certain he won't mind if you're a little late. He'll tell you which building. I'm on the third floor. Well, got to get back to work. I was out of black ink. Luckily for me, Burton's is close by."

"That's where I got my sketchpad," I told him.

In awe, I watched Mr. Liney go back over to speak with Matt. Occasionally, they looked over at me. I opened the paper to the comics section and locked my eyes on Henry, the bald-headed young boy, strolling and prancing across the panels without using words. There was no need for me to read, because the pictures told the story.

What would it take for me to become a real artist like John Liney? I wondered. There was so much I wanted to know and understand. *Could I do what he does for a living? Does Mr. Liney even know any Colored artists? Will I be too afraid to ask him?*

"Hey, Matt," I said at the end of the day, "do you mind if I drop in to see Mr. Liney tomorrow before I come to work?"

"That's fine," he responded. "Did he show you his *Henry* strip? John makes a pretty good living drawing."

"Did he say that he liked my sketches?"

"Sure did," said Matt. "John likes them just as much as me and your aunt Edna do."

The next afternoon, Vinny and I met up after school. "Guess what?" I said, as we walked toward Chelten Avenue. "Yesterday I met a professional artist."

"So?" Vinny responded.

I started speed-talking. "Have you ever seen the comic strip *Henry*? John Liney, the cartoonist, made those pictures. He invited me to his studio. It's right up the block from my newsstand. Can you believe it? Matt says Mr. Liney gets paid lots for his comic strip."

"Could *you* ever make money drawing?" said Vinny.

"I already do," I snapped back. "Five cents a drawing."

Vinny laughed. "A measly nickel?"

I shrugged. "Don't know if I'll ever make *real* money."

"I went to the Philadelphia Museum of Art once with my folks," said Vinny. "I was bored stiff!"

"Mrs. Miller told me about a Colored artist whose work is in that museum, but I've never been there. Got to cut now—I'm going to see Mr. Liney today."

This all happened during a time when there was much less fear about interacting with strangers, so I followed Matt's directions to the studio. After climbing the stairs to the third floor, I paused at the door with John Liney's name painted on it. Taking a deep breath, I knocked.

"Door's open," he called out.

His studio was large, with tall windows, allowing sunlight to pour in. Right away I felt at ease, like it was welcoming me in. I found him hunched over a square table. It didn't sit flat, but was tilted at an angle. Extending over it was a hooded light bulb on a long arm. I'd never seen a lamp or a desk like that before.

On the right side of his worktable was another, shorter table, its top covered with art supplies. There were small bottles of ink neatly placed in a row, alongside a rotating tray that held brushes, pens, and pencils, as well as a water jar. Everything was within arm's reach.

"Well, young man," said Mr. Liney, "have you ever been in an artist's studio?"

I watched as Mr. Liney dunked his brush into the water jar, dried the tip with a towel, and then placed it in the rotating tray.

"Yes," I say, "sort of. My dad had me help Mrs. Stouman, one of his customers. She designs hex signs. Mrs. Stouman mixes up bright colors and has me fill in the spaces that she marks. Her hex signs were hung on houses and barns all over Bucks County!"

"Sounds like great training to me," said Mr. Liney. "Now come over here and watch. This strip is due tomorrow. It's almost finished. Next, I'll ink the last panel."

I couldn't take my eyes off him. In his hand was a tool much like a paintbrush handle, but it had a metal tip. "This is a pen holder and nib. I can vary the weight of a line by changing the nib. And over here is my taboret," he added, referring to his supply table.

Laying his work aside, he pointed to a bunch of pencil sketches. "These are rough drawings," he explained. "This is where I work out ideas. Some work, others not so much," Mr. Liney added, winking at me as if he knew me.

"Dad has a worktable, too," I say, "but he hangs his tools on a wall, and his workplace is in the cellar."

"What does your father do?" Mr. Liney asked.

"He fixes things, builds and repairs furniture, paints and wallpapers houses, and sometimes sells vegetables and fruits from the back of our station wagon."

"Whoa," Mr. Liney responded. "That's a lot. What does he like doing best of all?"

"My dad," I said proudly, "likes making things with his hands."

Then Mr. Liney showed me around the rest of his studio, until finally he looked at his watch. "You should get to work now, young man. We can go over how I begin a strip on your next visit. Also, I want to know more about you and see more of your sketches. And I'd be pleased if from now on we call each other by first names. Run along now, Jerry."

I headed out, skipping stairs, and ran down the block.

"What's your hurry?" Matt called out as I grabbed my bundle of papers from him and started across the street. "How did it go?"

"You should see all the stuff John draws with—a whole lot more than pencils! And both of us buy supplies from Burton's. And he wants to see more of my sketches. And he even invited me to come back!"

After that and several more visits with John Liney, my bedroom became my studio. Mother and Dad gave me a desk to put in front of the small window in my room. I spent my pay on all kinds of art supplies and an oil-paint set. The dresser top became my taboret. The only thing I bought besides art supplies were soda pops and Clark bars.

I wanted my own paintings to match the shading in my pencil drawings, delicately rendered. I'd already begun to teach myself by looking at photos in magazines and copying images from the biblical calendar that hung from the hook on our living room wall. This month's image was of Jesus praying at a rock. After I copied it dozens of times, it would turn out to be my first oil painting.

Months later, after coming home from the newsstand, I discovered a brand-new tackle box sitting on top of the dresser, right next to the art supplies. *Where did this come from?* I wondered.

Mother had been quietly standing in the doorway. "Word on the avenue is, 'Buy a paper from Jerry, and he might draw you.' Your father bought you the tackle box," Mother said affectionately. "He thought you might be needing a place to keep your supplies, now that you're planning to study art when you go to high school."

At the beginning of the next school year, I would be headed to Murrell Dobbins Vocational High School to study commercial art. Dobbins was all the way across town in North Philly, which seemed like a world away. It would take two buses to get there, and for the first time, I would be going to school alone. But unlike before my first days at Roosevelt, I wasn't as anxious this time, because art was my safe space. At long last, I'd be able to center my art skills at school.

One afternoon after school Bobby called to me from the alley. I raised the window, and he said, "Jerry, me and the guys are headed to the gym. Want to come along?"

"Naw, man," I said. "Need to finish up this drawing."

Bobby frowned. "What do you think all this art stuff is going to get you?" he asked.

"I'm not sure," I responded, "but I'm going to give it a try."

"Well, I hope you get something out of all the time you're putting into it. You're really good at drawing. Everybody on Earlham Street says so."

I held my sketchpad up to the window. "I'll show you this one when it's finished."

Bobby smiled. "See ya!" he yelled as he ran down the alley.

I may have seemed confident, but Bobby's comment stuck with me. *I hope I'm going to get something out of all the time I'm putting into it, too.* Could I make it through high school and get a good job, even though I had so much trouble with reading? Could another Black artist like Henry

O. Tanner have a career and be recognized, as Mrs. Miller had said? Could I ever make a living making pictures—maybe even becoming well known—like John Liney?

I couldn't even begin to dream of my art being shown in a place like the Philadelphia Museum of Art. I'd never even *been* to a museum.

But all that time I'd put into drawing, I was drawing my dream. And one day, more than fifty years later, the Philadelphia Museum of Art mounted a solo exhibition titled *Witness: The Art of Jerry Pinkney.*

Mother had turned out to be right. She had always said that I would make something of my name.

Top: Jerry Pinkney as a boy.
Bottom: Graduation photo from
Dobbins Vocational High School.

WHAT HAPPENED NEXT

Meeting John Liney changed everything for me. After those visits, I started to believe in the possibility that my talents might lead to an actual profession. In order to reassure my father, I chose the commercial art course as a major at Murrell Dobbins Vocational High School. My dream was to acquire the skills to earn a livelihood and to learn what opportunities were available for a person who had a passion for drawing.

My teachers were well qualified in the practices and processes of art and design and brought purpose to my world of picture-making. Prior to entering Dobbins, I had no way as a person of color to comprehend a future in the arts—until I met Mr. Samuel Brown, a Black professional artist. Mr. Brown managed a sign shop as well and hired me as his apprentice. More than fifty years later, one of my paintings was acquired by the Philadelphia Museum of Art and included in a 2014 exhibition titled *Represent: Two Hundred Years of*

Paintings by Jerry Pinkney from his retellings of the Aesop fables *The Three Billy Goats Gruff* and *The Grasshopper & the Ants*.

African American Art at the Philadelphia Museum of Art—and to my surprise, I discovered it hanging on the same wall with a watercolor by my mentor, Samuel Brown.

Although Dobbins was an integrated school with both Black and white students, I wasn't always able to escape racial bias. The commercial art teacher in my senior year had a unique grade for what he perceived as exceptional artistry—an "A with wings"—and I received more A's with wings than any other student in his class. Yet, in 1957, when there was little opportunity for Black students to pursue the applied arts as a vocation, our teacher thought it best to give board of education scholarship forms to white students only. Determined not to be overlooked, I went to the guidance counselor's office and secured applications for both myself and the other Black students. That year, Philadelphia's board of education awarded three scholarships. Two

Paintings by Jerry Pinkney from his reimaginings of *Twinkle, Twinkle, Little Star* and Hans Christian Andersen's *The Little Mermaid*.

of them were given to Black students at Dobbins: one to my classmate and friend, Warren Neale, and the other to me.

I entered the Philadelphia Museum School of Art (now University of the Arts) majoring in advertising and design. Once again, my choice of this major was to show Dad that I was making every effort to use my education as a vehicle to lead to employment. After two and a half years at PMSA, I took a leave of absence, unsure if I could find a job after art school. With a need to provide for myself, I discovered an opening at a florist's downtown and was hired to deliver flowers. Not long afterward, I received a promotion to floral designer.

In 1960, I was referred to a position at Rust Craft Greeting Card Company in Dedham, Massachusetts, and after sharing my drawing portfolio, I was hired. Recently married, I moved to Boston with my wife, Gloria Jean, and our first child. Two years later I was invited to join Barker–Black, a design and illustration studio in Boston, as illustrator/designer. It was there that I illustrated my first children's book, *The Adventures of Spider* by Joyce Cooper Arkhurst, published by Little, Brown and Company in 1964. With that project I wove together two disciplines into a book—my passion for drawing and my proficiency in layout and design. Since then, I have illustrated more than one hundred books for children and many novels for adults.

This book was written to show young readers, and those with learning differences, how I became an artist against the odds. Hopefully all children with or without challenges will be encouraged and inspired to wonder if they can, too.

Left: Jerry with sisters Claudia and Helen.
Right: Jerry's oldest sister, Joan, at age seventeen.

Left: Brother Eddie in Navy uniform.
Right: Brother Billy in Air Force uniform.

The essence of the experiences in this book are true to how I best recall them, but not necessarily in the order that they occurred. To provide a cohesive snapshot of my early years for young readers, I have compressed, manipulated, or montaged some scenes and timelines, except for the details of working at the newsstand and meeting John Liney. Some names have been changed when memory failed, but none concerning family members, neighbors on East Earlham Street, friends, teachers, and mentors. What I will never forget is all the love shared, the spirit, and the positive yet chaotic energy of life lived on our dead-end block in Germantown, the historic section of Philadelphia, Pennsylvania.

The patchwork of chapters in this book represent key experiences and values that have made up my life narrative and influenced my path to becoming an artist. How often the subjects, experiences, and sense of place that originated in those childhood spaces have been a compass and inspiration for my work, whether it's the busy stimulation of East Earlham Street, the exuberant energy in a home that strained to accommodate a family of eight, the struggles I faced as a sensitive child who was easily overwhelmed by my learning challenges at school, or the continual shadow of racism hanging over my world beyond East Earlham Street.

My inner drive as a young Black boy trying to excel was rooted in the challenges of growing up with an at-the-time unnamed and poorly understood learning disability, and with the pain of feeling different. Trying to balance my battles with dyslexia and an inner need to be accepted and praised by the broader community was a daily struggle. Because reading was so difficult, drawing gave me an outlet to process reality, express myself, and dream of a world where I had more power and agency. Mrs. Miller's request for me to draw a fire engine for the class was a moment that forever seeded how I saw my own capacity to be in control and influence others with drawing. This book itself is a result of my desire to expand my creative capabilities through hard work and determination to fulfill another dream: to become a writer.

I learned about American history and the enslavement of Africans and their descendants through the lens of my Black teachers at Joseph E. Hill Elementary School. Within my work I have tried to visually interpret that time and place in a way that reflects the unwavering dignity radiating from my parents, as well as our rich, complex heritage and the enduring legacy of people of African descent (such as in *The Old African* by Julius Lester). While in the 1940s and 1950s people inside and outside the Black community referred to us as "Colored," I have chosen to use that word only in thoughts and dialogue, for accuracy. In today's society that term is no longer imbued with the sense of dignity that I witnessed and with which I was raised. Yet, I felt it important to use the term in order to truly immerse readers in the cultural landscape of my youth.

Despite my being surrounded by a loving family and neighbors, living in the shadow of the Jim Crow laws that my parents and other Southern families on East Earlham Street had tried to flee was never easy, and it was an often silent but heavy weight on the grownups as well as on their children. Drawing became my refuge.

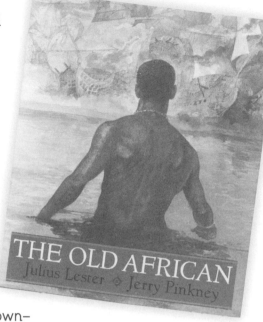

Western movies were also an escape for me, as well as a catalyst to think about the world outside our dead-end block in Germantown. What a revelation it was as an adult to learn that one out of every four cowboys was Black or Mexican. Much later in life, I learned about the problematic aspects of the "cowboy hero" in relationship to Indigenous people who were often treated as enemies or as "other." Yet, even with my limited knowledge of these cultures, I always felt a connection with Indigenous peoples and their way of honoring wildlife and the land. In 1970, I accepted an assignment from the National Park Service in

collaboration with the New York Society of Illustrators to create watercolors on the Nez Perce Reservation in Idaho. For me it fostered a renewed and deeper interest in America's Indigenous peoples. As a result, that year I illustrated *Tonweya and the Eagles and Other Lakota Tales* by Rosebud Yellow Robe. This is just one example of how the books I choose to illustrate have always been motivated by my personal experiences.

This interest and passion for the natural world, ever present in my art, stem directly from visits to Aunt Helen's and Uncle Osbie's New Jersey farm, and I treasured those open-air sojourns from the city. I had always loved living things and didn't even like killing insects; the accidental death of the bird solidified my reverence for animal life. It was always emotionally challenging for me to visit a zoo, where animals were locked in cages, nor did I enjoy going to the circus. How grateful I am to have worked on many animal fable retellings, such as *The Lion and the Mouse*, which provided an artistic sanctuary for me to pay homage to animal life of all kinds.

My relationship with Mother and Dad provided the building blocks for all I achieved. Mother gave daily support. She was my muse, anchor, and balance. The memory of my mother, Williemae, reading aloud Aesop's Fables and stories of Hans Christian Andersen such as "The Ugly Duckling" and "The Little

Mermaid" fed my interest in classic storytelling. And how powerful it was for me to grow up surrounded by the menfolk telling tall tales, such as the story of hero John Henry, in the oral Southern tradition.

Dad ingrained in me creative sensibilities, grit, and tenacity, and an appreciation for the value of handmade objects. The extent of his interest in my career didn't reveal itself, though, until I was twenty-eight, when Gloria Jean, our four children, and I were living in Boston, Massachusetts. Dad was spending time with us after Mother's passing. My converted studio was on the fourth floor of our South End row house. Dad rarely visited that studio and never inquired about my work. He showed no interest in the art-making process—or so I thought.

One day I noticed that some things in my studio had been moved out of place. After a while, we surmised that Dad had been climbing the stairs to my studio when everyone was sleeping. So I began laying out projects that I wanted him to see. I wondered what he was feeling; Dad never spoke a word to me about my work. Years later, when talking to my sisters about Dad, I mentioned that he had never expressed pride in what his son had accomplished. How surprised and pleased I was to hear about his returns from those Boston visits,

Jerry Pinkney's parents, James and Williemae Pinkney, on Earlham Street.

when time and again Claudia, Helen, and Joan had to listen to Dad's boasting about "his son Jerry, the artist." Looking back, I wonder: Was Dad as fascinated with my studio as I was with his basement workshop?

As quietly supportive as my parents were of my skill, given the daily needs required for raising six children on a modest income, they did not recognize the fact that art has the potential to transform lives. There was no time for museums or art gallery outings. As a result, I didn't visit a museum until PMSA's freshman class field trip to the Philadelphia Museum of Art. It was love at first sight. Once inside that seemingly infinite space framed by those massive stone columns, I discovered a universe that I could never have dreamed of. It was a world unrecognizable, but at the same time familiar. My eighteen-year-old self was mesmerized, transfixed by the expanse of paintings, sculptures, and medieval armor galleries stretching the imagination.

At last, I had a sense of belonging.

The Philadelphia Museum School of Art and the Philadelphia Museum of Art became artistic pathways to my future. In 1992, the University of the Arts presented me with the Alumni Award, and a few years later I was a recipient of a UA ARTS Silver Star Alumni Award. In 2013, PMA featured

The front cover of Jerry Pinkney's retelling of the Aesop fable *The Lion & the Mouse.*

the solo exhibition titled *Witness*. This show was exhibited and toured by the Norman Rockwell Museum of Art of Stockbridge, Massachusetts. In 2014, the jacket illustration for the book *John Henry* (written by Julius Lester) was acquired by the Philadelphia Museum of Art, and for my eighty-first birthday they posted a shout-out on their Instagram page. What a transformation this institution underwent in my life—from an unknown backdrop I'd speed by in my biking trips downtown with my buddies, to becoming a linchpin of my career.

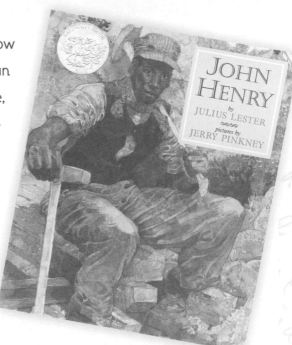

My evolution to professional creative started in Boston, Massachusetts, with Gloria Jean, my high school sweetheart and soulmate. There began our journey of friendship, love, collaborations, and the raising of our four children. Because of my experience as the lone artist in my Philadelphia family, we knew how important it was to expose our children to the creative and performing arts. All four of them grew up to work in creative areas, and some of our grandchildren are following suit.

Oftentimes Dad could be heard saying, "Life can be beautiful!" And for me, having the opportunity to pursue my passion and share it with children for so many decades, it most certainly has been just that: beautiful.

Jerry Pinkney (top right) in the 1970s with his family,
from left: Gloria Jean, Troy, Myles (top), Brian, and Scott.

Jerry Pinkney

KEY DATES AND SELECT ACCOMPLISHMENTS

1939 Born December 22.

1952 Graduates from Joseph E. Hill Elementary School.

1953 Graduates from Theodore Roosevelt Junior High School.

1957 Graduates from Murrell Dobbins Career & Technical Education High School, also known as Murrell Dobbins Vocational High School.

1957–60 Attends the University of the Arts in Philadelphia (previously Philadelphia Museum School of Art).

1960 Marries Gloria Jean Maultsby.

1960 Begins working at the Rust Craft Greeting Card Company.

1962–64 Works at Barker–Black Studio.

1964 First children's book illustrations published in *The Adventures of Spider: West African Folktales* by Joyce Cooper Arkhurst.

1968 Begins Jerry Pinkney Studio.

1977 Iconic jacket illustration for Mildred D. Taylor's Newbery Medal–winning *Roll of Thunder, Hear My Cry* is published.

1981 Receives a Coretta Scott King Honor for *Count on Your Fingers African Style* by Claudia Zaslavsky.

1986 Wins the Coretta Scott King Award for *The Patchwork Quilt* by Valerie Flournoy.

1987 Wins the Coretta Scott King Award for *Half a Moon and One Whole Star* by Crescent Dragonwagon.

1989 Receives a Caldecott Honor and wins the Coretta Scott King Award for *Mirandy and Brother Wind* by Patricia McKissack.

1990 Receives a Caldecott Honor and Coretta Scott King Honor for *The Talking Eggs* by Robert D. San Souci.

1992 First collaboration with Gloria Jean Pinkney, the picture book *Back Home*, is published.

1992 Honored with the Alumni Award from the University of the Arts in Philadelphia (previously Philadelphia Museum School of Art).

1993 Receives the Alumni Award from Murrell Dobbins Career & Technical Education High School.

1995 Receives a Caldecott Honor for *John Henry* by Julius Lester.

1997 Wins a Coretta Scott King Award for *Minty: A Story of Young Harriet Tubman* by Alan Schroeder.

1997 Wins a *New York Times* Best Illustrated Children's Books Award for *The Hired Hand: An African-American Folktale* by Robert D. San Souci.

1998 Nominated for the Hans Christian Andersen Award for Illustration.

2000 Receives a Caldecott Honor for *The Ugly Duckling* by Hans Christian Andersen.

2000 Wins the Virginia Hamilton Literary Award from Kent State University.

2002 Wins a Coretta Scott King Award for *Goin' Someplace Special* by Patricia McKissack.

2003 Receives a Caldecott Honor and the Sydney Taylor Book Award Honor for *Noah's Ark*, written and illustrated by Jerry Pinkney.

2003 Appointed to the National Council of the Arts (NEA). Serves from 2003 to 2009.

2003 Receives an Honorary Doctorate of Fine Arts from the Art Institute of Boston at Lesley University.

2003 Receives the Outstanding Learning Disabled Achievers Award from The Lab School of Washington.

2004 Awarded the University of Southern Mississippi Medallion for outstanding contributions in the field of children's literature.

2005 Receives a Coretta Scott King Honor for *God Bless the Child* by Billie Holiday and Arthur Herzog Jr.

2005–06 *Illuminated Literature: The Art of Jerry and Brian Pinkney* exhibits at the Morris Museum of Art.

2006 Receives the Original Art Lifetime Achievement Award from the Society of Illustrators.

2009 Receives a Coretta Scott King Honor for *The Moon Over Star* by Dianna Hutts Aston.

2009 Wins a *New York Times* Best Illustrated Children's Books Award for *The Lion & The Mouse*.

2010 Wins the Caldecott Medal for *The Lion & the Mouse*.

2010 Receives a Doctorate of Fine Arts, honoris causa, from the Pennsylvania College of Art and Design.

2010 Awarded the Liberty Bell Citation by the City of Philadelphia.

2011 Inducted into the Society of Illustrators Hall of Fame.

2011 Nominated for the Astrid Lindgren Memorial Award.

2012 Inducted into the American Academy of Arts & Sciences.

2012 Receives an honorary Doctorate of Humane Letters from the Bank Street Graduate School of Education in New York.

2013 *Witness: The Art of Jerry Pinkney* exhibit is organized by the Norman Rockwell Museum.

2013 Receives the Distinguished Arts Award at the Governor's Awards for the Arts in Pennsylvania.

2014 Named a Carle Honors honoree by the Eric Carle Museum of Picture Book Art.

2016 Receives a Coretta Scott King–Virginia Hamilton Award for Lifetime Achievement.

2016 Wins the Laura Ingalls Wilder Award (renamed the Children's Literature Legacy Award).

2016 *Jerry Pinkney: Imaginings: An Artist's Explorations of Images and Words* exhibit is organized by the Norman Rockwell Museum.

2017 Receives a Coretta Scott King Honor for *In Plain Sight* by Richard Jackson.

2017 *The Storybook Magic of Jerry Pinkney* exhibits at the Woodmere Art Museum.

2018 Receives the Norton Juster Award for Devotion to Literacy.

2019 *Freedom's Journal: The Art of Jerry Pinkney* exhibits at the Woodmere Art Museum.

2021 Dies October 20.

2022 *Tenacity & Resilience: The Art of Jerry Pinkney* exhibits at the Montclair Art Museum.